MAGIC

MINDSET & MANIFESTATIONS

A PRACTICAL AND SPIRITUAL GUIDE TO

Manifesting Your Dream Life

LUCI MCMONAGLE

Published by Luci McMonagle
Luci McMonagle
Chandler, Arizona

For ordering information or special discounts for bulk purchases, please contact Luci McMonagle

Picture images are under the Creative Commons CC0, most are from pxhere.com. Graphics were created for this book commissioned by Luci.

First Edition

ISBN: 978-1-7343785-0-4

Library of Congress Control Number: 2019920717

Disclaimer

The author has designed the information to be presented as her opinion on its content. As the reader, it is your responsibility to do your own research and due diligence to determine if any advice is right for your circumstances. All of the recommendations suggested are an opinion. The advice contained in this book may not be suitable for you or your situation. It is not a substitute for professional advice from a Certified Financial Planner, Mental Health Professional or any other type of professional field. You should always use common sense and your best judgment to determine if something is right for you or not. The author is not in the business of giving legal, financial, accounting, mental health or any other type of professional advice. She does not offer any representations, warranties or guarantees, verbally or in writing, regarding your earnings or results. You alone are responsible for your actions and results in life and business without any claims to the author or this content. The solutions presented in this book have worked for the author and the clients she has served. They may work for you too.

Book Dedication

With deepest gratitude for my family whom without them, this book would not have been possible. A special dedication to my son, David, and my grandson, Dyson who has given me the strength to break the cycle to go for more.

And I would like to dedicate this book to you, the reader. Without you, it would not be possible for me to reach out to the world and, together, make it a better place. I deeply and profoundly appreciate what you have done and will do to create a life that you feel is a phenomenal success.

Please Share this with others and consider creating your own book club.

I am deeply and profoundly grateful for every single person who has ever touched my soul and my heart, as it has made this book possible through my life experiences. There are so many of you that I would have to write another book to list you all. Abundant blessings and thanks for providing me with insight, acknowledgement, support, dedication, and, most of all, my life's experiences.

Meet the Author

Luci McMonagle is a natural born intuitive medium, mentor and trained energy worker and healer. She can answer your questions through medium-ship, explain your Soul Purpose through a face analysis, Activate and Align Your Twelve Chakras, and offer you gifts from Spirit, energy balls and other fun energetic energies to help you on your journey. Luci has 10 spirit gift markings that give her the powerful ability to help you through deep emotional transitions and getting you unstuck while she accesses deep inner wisdom and dimensions of consciousness. She is a Clairvoyant, a Gifted Healer and is a Master Practitioner of Psychosomatic.

Luci has been providing intuitive readings, teaching classes and providing healings and energy work since the 1990's. She was a regular reader at the Psychic Fairs created by the Inner Peace Foundation in Green Bay, Wisconsin. She's also have been trained in the healing arts, was a resident healer at the White Star Psychic Science Church and worked at Wonewoc Spiritualist Camp. Luci has been professionally trained in the development of her natural born gifts and is ordained as a Spiritualist. She continues to provide intuitive readings, creates classes and provides energy work at Vision Quest Metaphysical Bookstore in Phoenix, Arizona. She has created events, classes, seminars, given tens of thousands of readings, blessings, and helped others. She is a true Mystic and is a catalyst for your deep level transformations.

This book will provide you with valuable healing, blessings and practical tools that will transform you life if you use them.

FROM RAGS TO RICHES

Luci transformed the poverty-stricken life she grew up in to a life of abundance, wealth, and happiness. Luci has created millions in her life while working part-time by Mastering the Practical & Spiritual aspects of Wealth Manifestations. Her unique approach of blending spirituality with practicality will remove your hidden blocks to success and help increase your money while having more fun.

Luci is a highly sought after Mystic, Spiritual Teacher, Professional Speaker, and International Best Selling Author. She will empower you to take your current situation and turn it into a satisfying, wealthy and harmonious one. Her work is known to bring miracles and magic!

> This book has been specifically created to activate your wealth vibes and get you unstuck. This activation is from high vibrational words placed in a sequence that gets to the root of your sabotages, heal your emotional wounds and starts to unfold a deeper sense of inner peace and faith from within you.

“May you find peace in your heart
and healing to your soul.”

Luci's soul purpose is to calm souls down so they can receive activations, healings and messages from their spirit guides and guardian angels. Luci channels the divine universal truths, downloads the harmonic codes and brings into the world the light codes for awakening humanity.

She is on a personal life mission to cultivate freedom and power in people's lives by awakening their courage, their insights, and wisdom to transform into their own greatness so that they have a lightness of being.

This book is designed to empower you to take the first steps toward attracting miracles into your own life.

TESTIMONIES

*"You want someone to tell you who you are.
I mean who you really are? Some wouldn't.
It's a great way for someone else to point out
your strengths and weaknesses so you can work
on being a better person. If you're looking for
someone to read you, I mean really tell you
who you are, you've got to give
Luci McMonagle a try."*

~Mitchell Levy, MBA

~~~~~

*"Luci is an AMAZING person whom I am
privileged to know! My first call with Luci was a
clearing she did on me and OH WOW!!! The
things she hit were spot on! Then nearly a year
later Luci and I started to work together. She
could literally feel my energy from a distance!
This blew me away as I would be winning at life
and get a text from Luci saying, Congrats or
something inspiring for me. It's like she knew a
new client signed on with me :) I HIGHLY
recommend Luci to anyone who is looking to
increase their awareness and take their business
and personal mindset to a higher level!!"*

~Denise Dominguez
~~~~~

"I highly recommend Luci to anyone who's ready to express their fullest potential in the world just by tapping into their own greatness! Thank you Luci!"

~Merry Paul

~~~~~

"I read Luci's first book 2 times in a 3 day period. The first time I simply read it. The second time I performed the activities. Here's the crazy part - 3 days later. I got a small check in the mail. The next day another small check arrived. Day 3 I woke up almost six thousand dollars in my account."

"I recommend this book for it's amazing value. If you do as prescribed in the activities you will see results."

~Amazon Customer for
Magical Money Manifestations.
~~~~~

TABLE OF CONTENTS

Summary

This book is designed to activate your greatness with intuition and divine wisdom. It will benefit you to use a journal alongside this book for optimal results. *Magic, Mindset and Manifestations* is the upgraded version of her first International Best Selling Book, *Magical Money Manifestations*.

> **This book is encoded with a sequence of high-vibration words and energy that can trigger lighter states of being from within you.**

As you move through each chapter, you may feel a sense of movement that you might not be able to explain. This is normal. You may experience emotions and feelings that come up for no apparent reason. Allow the feelings to come to the surface so you can let them go. Start paying attention to your life, the world, and the influences around you. Be mindful when it appears that something is falling apart. It is actually a sure sign that everything is starting to fall into place for your greater good.

What may first appear as chaos is a form of divine order that is taking place in your life. Rushing through this book will not fully benefit you, but if you must skip ahead, please be sure to go back to the beginning and go through this in sequence, or you may experience skewed results. Take your time to explore this journey and enjoy the process as you go through it. When something comes up that you label as bad, reframe your thinking to look at the circumstances as something very interesting instead. Writing in a journal to document your transformation will allow you to enjoy the process with a bit more ease and grace. Abundant blessings, and may your journey to greatness begin today.

A NOTE ABOUT PERSONAL GAIN

If your money and wealth was to increase, what would you do?

How would you spend your time?

Would you do more or less good because you are wealthy?

With all that time would you buy things for yourself and for other people?

Would you look at the world differently if you knew that you could have anything you desired?

You have a choice to use your wealth as a force of good or not. When you have more than enough, you are able to help yourself, your family, and the world at large.

Money is energy and energy needs to circulate. When you use money affirm you are recirculating it and it will return back to you.

When you have more, you give more, when you create more wealth and abundance for yourself, you naturally create more wealth and abundance for other people. When you choose to empower yourself, you give hope to others that feel disempowered. You have the power to change your world and the world around you. This book will get you started on how.

So I say to you. Personal gain is a good thing, you are a good person and when you increase your wealth, whether it's monetary wealth, information wealth, or other forms of wealth - you will increase the wealth of others. This creates a stimulation of the economy and everybody wins because of the circulation of energy and this energy always recirculates.

Chapter 1

THE INNER HUNGER

First, let me state that Magic and Manifestations are a skill that anyone can learn, including you. Yes! I do mean a skill that can be proven by science. These skills are scientific because they are repeatable, duplicable, and teachable. This means that you can learn this just as you learned how to read and write. This entire book has all the information you need to get started. It is not the complete guide for you, but it will get you well on the way to creating a life of your dreams. It has the basic necessary elements and much more. Reading this entire book straight through and not skipping around will yield you the best results. If you jump around trying this and that or saying to yourself that you already know that, you might not be able to fully reach your ultimate potential. Making the Decree that You Tried That ONCE and at the time it did not yield you the results, does not mean that it will not work now. This mindset will keep you in a prison that you never know you are in. So, catch yourself when you start to say, I know that. I tried that and it didn't work. These will keep you exactly where you are - not where you want to go.

> **Start with a new intention and fresh open mind and heart as you go through this book. It will manifest miracles for you.**

If you skip through this book and read parts of it, you may still manifest, but the results may be wacky. So, if you currently are not yet at a six-figure plus income, then definitely do not skip ahead.

There is a sequence of high-vibration and magical words encoded throughout this book that is designed to trigger awakenings and unleash your deep inner hidden magic.

These encodings are set up in a sequence and as you flow through each chapter another layer of energy that has been keeping you stuck will start losing its grip on you.

This book is set up as an "activation" for you and as a process that will make this transition go as smoothly as possible for you.

- ✓ It will benefit you to use a journal or notepad alongside this book to practice the exercises and for taking notes.

Let me begin by talking about that gnawing feeling you may have been ignoring for far too long, and then we will get into your seeds of greatness that are getting ready to sprout.

Deep inside us, we have a hunger; some kind of need that we cannot seem to fulfill or satisfy. We search endlessly, trying to fill this empty void, until we have exhausted ourselves and our resources. We run in circles, making ourselves dizzy with desire, but never finding anything that will make this deep-seated need become satisfied or fulfilled. After long periods searching, we tend to collapse from the sheer force of gravity.

You may wonder:

What exactly happened...?

Why have my efforts not been appreciated...?

Why have I not been valued...?

Why is everybody else continuing to take from me even when I feel I have nothing left to give...?

There seems to be no return on your investments, no food that will satisfy you, and no drink that will quench your thirst.

You may try to block out this hunger because you simply do not know what you are missing that is creating this feeling. Maybe you've tried loving until your heart was shattered. Or you have given of yourself until there was nothing else to give. Perhaps you've stood for a cause and battled fights you never even started.

Where can relief be found? Perhaps you've already looked to God, the world, your family, your loved ones. You left no stone unturned, no region unexplored, and yet here you are feeling unappreciated. You might even feel like you've been abandoned by everything and let down by everybody. A part of you might feel so angry you can barely stand it, yet you are too afraid to open your mouth out of fear that you appear like a crazy person. Because you fear once you start you won't be able to stop. Or perhaps you feel so helpless and alone that no one could understand why you keep giving and are always feeling alone. You might even fear that if you tolerate just one more disappointment, you will go on a rampage that will end in terror and tears.

How do you find the strength to carry on? Who can you turn to? Is there anybody even there for if you fall? Can you only rely on yourself? There is an endless sea of questions that you might force yourself to ask simply to avoid the emptiness. Or maybe you cram every waking minute with busyness and noise; noise that you hope will shut out this horrible feeling that you are sure nobody else could possibly understand or experience. There does not appear to be any reason for this emptiness or hunger.

The truth is that you may be so afraid of looking inside yourself to explore this feeling that you direct all of your energy outside of yourself with deep resentment when your expectations are not met. Sometimes you may even pretend as if it does not exist and hope that if you do not notice it, it will go away.

Finding the missing pieces that are causing this deep void inside you can be an easier journey than you might think. This void is missing pieces of your soul and your sacred heart. You will become one again with your authentic self if you are willing to put in the work. And please note that the work can be done with ease and grace. It can be completed as an exploration into the unseen while having a fabulously wonderfully good time. You see, in all honesty, I thought that the only way I could get ahead in life was if I was serious all of the time. But in truth you can easily access your seeds of greatness with less than half of the effort it has taken you to prevent it.

This book is designed to start the process with you - not for you. And the great part is that even if you just decide to read through this book without doing many of the explorations or exercises, you will be farther along than most people. Now start awakening.

I understand the pain you are going through. I felt it myself for many years. This book will help you to truly unleash your inner self and I will explain some secrets I have discovered. These secrets will empower you to start creating magical manifestations in your life. Perhaps you can identify with this as I start to discuss your seeds of greatness.

I understand that being a kind-hearted, loving individual can be difficult if you have fears that others will not like you. You might agonize over "how" you can be accepted, liked and how you can help. You may look for ways to fix other people, give advice, direct and get down right annoyed by those you might even call "Sheeple." It's frustrating to be waking up in a world that still seems to be sleeping. The root cause of all of this is bable. Bable meaning that you along with everyone else has not been taught that first there is thought, then word, then action. You may not have been taught that your words are powerful beyond measure. You were probably taught not to trust your intuition, instinct or self. When you got hurt when you were younger, you were probably told the pain wasn't that bad. Or maybe you were told that you were "too sensitive" as if it was a bad thing to have feelings.

Right now the world as a whole is facing a time of great change and many individuals do not know what to do about it. As caregivers of the Earth you and I have the power to make this world a better place. Just one person can start an entire movement that changes the world. One person can be the one that ends the family generational curses and karmic debt. Just one person.

And That One Person Can Be You!

This book can help you start accessing Your Seeds of Greatness that have been calling from the depths of your soul.

The truth has been hidden from you because in the process of helping others "First," you somehow forgot about yourself. You've given others your money, time and energy. You've met others along your life's journey who took advantage of your kind nature. Sometimes this was intentional, but most of the time it was simply misguided and misdirected aspects of a wounded soul who yearned for healing. Their wound found your wound and for a moment, there may have been a sense of belonging – as if for a brief moment – You were "Understood."

Yes, as a whole, we go about our daily lives, our wounds are covered up with our busyness and, eventually, we even forget they were there to begin with. Our wound started well before we became adults. We forgot ourselves in the maze of growing up and we forgot our pains, leaving Band-Aids on our scars until those were just forgotten too. We began to focus on surviving our life and growing up. We would take care of daily cares, chores, others, the house, and the car, creating endless lists of things needing our attention. Every time we took a moment for ourselves, we were nudged, berated, and told we were selfish. Or worse yet, we told ourselves that. Even though it was unnatural for us to ignore the aches and pains of our emotional and physical body, we learned to pretend it was not as important as other's needs. You may have this driving force to want to change the world. You may have this deep yearning that something has to give. But you may not know what that something is.

After many years of sleep deprivation and struggling, we begin to feel empty and wonder what this void is inside of us. We try to cover it up with another Band-Aid, but that just falls off and the sting hits harder. Eventually, our emotional and physical bodies start to scream at us until we can no longer dull the pain. You may be experiencing this dull aching pain, but you have not been able to put your finger on it.

This deep inner feeling may have you looking for answers everywhere and you may feel disappointed because you have not found them yet. The things that are beyond what used to be our comfort zone will start to slip away. In the past, as a collective, we have been sliding up and down our inner comfort zones. If you have had lower lows and higher highs, then you will be relieved to know that things are about to change for you. Even if you feel like you are having a breakdown. You may be getting ready to have a breakthrough on several levels. Sometimes the only way to move forward is to hit the bottom and feel stagnate. Then, after the discomfort becomes too much for you, you may have started trudging upwards again. Then you may have hit a plateau and bounced down again. This was once the normal for me. It may feel like an emotional roller coaster cycle for you too. You may have been so frustrated and yelled out to the Universe: "What is going on?!" If you have felt this frustrated and sometimes have fallen into apathy, this book may help you find the answers to these questions and more. Keep on reading. Move through each chapter, even if it seems that somehow your life has been confused with the law of gravity saying: "What goes up, must come down."

There is hope and a path to freedom.

Once you start pulling out the seeds of doubt, fear, and hopelessness, you will have room to plant seeds of greatness within your mental garden. I am here to help you do that, if you are willing and ready. I know that, if you are still reading, you are ready to start creating a life that is filled with magic, freedom, and joy. You will be able to start living your true inner passions; the ones you forgot so long ago that it may seem like an old forgotten memory. I am going to take you through a process in this book. This process has been used by hundreds with miraculous results, and now it is available to you.

"Hope… sometimes that's all you have
when you have nothing else. If you have It.
You have everything."

In this moment, your life is changing. Your decision to search for something that has a deeper meaning and your desire to want more are in fact changing your life in the most wonderful ways.

Have you ever had that feeling, a deep down gnawing feeling; that there is something beneath the surface? Have you ever laid awake at night feeling afraid and desiring that feeling to go away? You do not want to keep experiencing this over and over again. You want things to be different, but you do not know how. You are bumping against a financial glass ceiling or some other wall. Sometimes, you might even justify that you are really not that unhappy about your circumstances, but you really do not feel inspired to change that much either. You really cannot quite figure out why you have this feeling. You sense there is something wrong but, in all appearances, you cannot see anything wrong. You do not really think you should be doing something different, but you still have that feeling.

After a while you finally get some relief, because that feeling goes away. That is, for a little while anyway. Then it seems to come back stronger and more persistent than the last time. It keeps happening over and over, and you feel this is like ocean waves in slow motion. The feeling comes over you and you feel overwhelmed as if you are drowning. Then it subsides and goes back so you can catch your breath; then it comes back to get even stronger and more powerful than it was before.

I want you to know that it is okay. I want you to understand that this is your true essence coming to the surface. And all of us has been well programmed to ignore this. We have been trained to be afraid of trying new things, of dreaming too big. You are afraid your parents will look at you as the person who dreamed too big and feel disappointed as if they failed.

The thing you fear the most is failure yet, you may also fear too much success too. It's really weird isn't it? You don't want to fail, but if you succeed too great, then that scares the heck out of you too? I certainly know this feeling. When things would start getting "too good" for me, I would suddenly start looking for the shoe to drop, the next problem that would crop up. I feared for my life, at times, that if I became too successful, the fall would be that much farther down? That I would spiral down a bottomless pit and would lose everything I worked so hard to accomplish.

Saint Teresa of Avila said,
"There are more tears shed over answered prayers then over unanswered prayers."

And so I would fear my prayers, affirmations or magic would be unanswered, but a part of me would also fear that they would be answered. This is a frustrating place to be. Because my heart would be saying yes, yes, yes and my mind would say no, no, no - what if!

This is a form of self torture in my opinion and I was becoming a pro at it by the time I was in my early twenties. This state lasted for me until my mid forties. And then I learned how to make my heart and mind in agreement! This was truly a game changer for me. Now, please note, I had to do the following exercise several times daily at first. Then, I was able to get it down to a few times a week. Then, to a few times a month. Now, I complete it about once every month or two for maintenance or when I start to notice when my head is going in one direction and my heart in another direction.

Are you ready to stop being beside yourself and playing tug of war with yourself?

Awesome! Mark this page for easy reference in the future or write this down in your journal.

Mind and Heart in Agreement Exercise

Get into a comfortable sitting position. Place your feet flat on the ground and your arms uncrossed.

Take a few deep breaths all the way down to your toes and let go of everything that prevents you from becoming relaxed. After you've done this several times and you feel relatively relaxed. Place one hand on your forehead and one hand on your chest area. It does not matter which hand goes where. Now breathe into your heart and ask for your heart and mind; your intellect and emotions to be in agreement and for this agreement to be cemented together so you are never besides yourself again.

Take a few more deep breaths and allow yourself to start becoming congruent in this area so you will be able to speak your truth with love and compassion.

You can now remove your hands from your mind and heart area and go about your day as usual. If you notice your mind and heart going in different directions, do this exercise again.

It's best to only start with small agreements. If you do this just once or twice and then expect to make a huge leap and be totally in agreement on major affairs, you may be setting yourself up for a disappointment. Be gentle on yourself as you've been an A plus student of life that has taught you how to doubt your heart and favor logic over emotions.

Keep doing this exercise. You can schedule it in your cell phone calendar or jot it down if you use a hand scheduler. This way you will be able to remember to do this. Before long, you will start to notice decisions start to come easier for you. Now it's not always going to be super easy to make every decision without some internal struggle. If you are like me, then, you may have some hidden beliefs inside of you that make some decisions more difficult than others. Or you may have some type of karma or contract with another person that needs to be fulfilled and you are blindsided by this.

Even at times when you may feel like you are not being fully successful in making good decisions, you did not fail. You have to understand that there truly is no failure. You might go on, or you might decide halfway through it that this is not what you really want. I am giving you permission to understand that it is alright. It is alright for you to be true to yourself. I give you permission to understand that if somebody else tells you that you are not making the right decisions or tells you that you should do this or that, be very leary. This person may mean well, but this person is also trying to place their limiting beliefs on you.

As an example, I was in the process of dating and also had some very good prospects for my business to increase my income. A "helpful friend" told me that I have to go for the money and give up on dating. My mind was like, What? Really, What do you mean can't date to find my life long partner and have a successful career or business? It was at that moment I realized this limitation was theirs and not mine. I thanked this person for their suggestion and stated in a matter of fact tone, that, I want it all and I can have it too.

If you have "helpful friends or family" like this, remember, it's not about you. It's not a limitation they see for you, but for them or through tainted thinking.

You might consider moving away from those kind of people or at the very least spend as little time with them as possible. You may need to re-evaluate your friends. You might need to limit your time with family members too and really learn not to take things personally. Not that you have to give up on them all, but do know that when you start improving your life, some may get jealous, others will feel betrayed or abandoned because you are not "like" them anymore, therefore, you don't "like" them either.

Be mindful when you are near anyone and you feel your energy drained away. You may be by an energy vampire.

Not everything will work out as you planned and you may tell yourself that perhaps so and so was correct. Maybe they were right and you were wrong. Don't beat yourself up over perceived failures. There is more to life than having everything turn out the way you expect it would.

Look at it from this perspective: *"What have I learned and how can I use this to create the dreams that I really want?"*

Look at how your soul has learned. How you've grown. A few of the hardest things we learn on a soul level is temperance - which is learning the exact opposite of what you want. This helps you to appreciate what you have when you find the balance. This is like a pendulum swinging from one extreme to the other until you figure out how to slow it down to the middle where you have a balanced viewpoint. The second hardest thing we learn on a soul level is strength. Strength is good to have and when you crumble and buckle to the point where you may be on your knees crying so hard you can't stand up, eventually, you find the resolve to make a decision to rebuild yourself the way you want to be. With the rebuilding of yourself, your strength is now stronger than ever. And usually you have more resolve to withstand what you have coming towards you.

Exercise: Grab your journal or notebook and your favorite writing tool or write in the boxes provided.

✍ Take about five to fifteen minutes to write down a couple of the things that did not work out how you wanted them to work out.

Now, with an open mind, ask yourself:

"Did something better come out of this?"

"What did I learn from this?"

"How am I using this knowledge to create something better?"

"How has this improved some aspect of my life?"

It is very important right now for you to understand that, sometimes your expectations are so narrowly defined. That you decided you had a negative experience because things didn't turn out exactly the way you wanted or as expected. You are completely focused on that negativity and you are completely focused on "Well, I must be a failure because it did not turn out the way I wanted it to turn out."

This type of Mindset will sabotage your ability to become successful. The mind is very clever at trying to keep you safe from real and imagined harms; you have to be careful about making expectations so narrow that you cannot see the beauty of what is really going on. Your life is starting to unfold in mysterious ways. Look for beautiful things and you will find them. Look for ugly things and you will find them.

What you choose to focus on will expand and grow. You will get more of it. So choose where you focus wisely. Not to say you can't have a negative day, a blow out when you are angry. It means on a daily base, pay attention to find hidden lies you believe about yourself that distort your life.

I have noticed that the people who have lives that they do not enjoy are focused on all of the things they do not like. Some people focus on their bodily aches and pains. All of us have pains and aches from our bodies. The key to managing your mindset is using this as a motivating factor, rather than as a deterrent, to moving forward in life.

Keep in mind that what you perceive is not necessarily what is real or even what is really going on. Ask your Guides, Angels, God, Creator, Higher Self or whatever you deem is a greater source for you to start seeing the larger picture than what you are currently seeing, because you probably have been trained to have blinders on and you only see a very small percentage of what is truly happening.

Now we are going to dive a bit deeper. I want to start by asking you a very deep yet very simple question:

"Are you really ready to make a difference in YOUR life?"

I do not mean by making a difference in someone else's life. You are an ace at doing that. What I am talking about is something that, generally speaking, we have been taught is selfish, self-centered, or other criticisms that may have been taught to you.

My goal is to educate you so you will be able to learn the difference between giving from a place of depletion and giving from the spaciousness of abundance. When you are in the space of overflowing abundance, you are more capable to give to others. This means that you give to yourself first until you are full and then, from there, you will be able to give to others.

I know you have what it takes and I know you will be able to make a huge difference to your future. Even if you are just starting out, even if you are only taking a baby step today - just one small step; stop for a moment and think of these questions:

Do you have or will you develop the mindset to carry you through, even when you think you are going to break?

What exactly are you looking for?

How do you want your future to be?

If you had absolutely nothing that could stop you... If money was no object... If a home, friends, family, obligations, or anything else could not stop you... If nothing could prevent you from getting what you truly want from life...:

What would you want your life to be like?

How would you feel?

What are you willing to do to go from where you are now to where you desire to be in life?

Notice I did not ask you HOW are you going to get to where you desire to be. Leave the specific how's up to magic and the universe. You can have a general how and do course corrections as you move closer to the dream life you are starting to choose to design.

Now, I know you have probably done a ton of work and you probably had more roadblocks than anybody else you ever knew. I know that your journey has been agonizing at times. I know how you feel. You are frustrated and you feel desolate at times. I know you may have already been on your knees crying so hard that you could not even stand. I have been there too. From the deepest parts of my being, I understand.

I am holding your hand right now. Just take a moment, close your eyes, and feel my hand very gently holding onto yours. I am encouraging you and I am here for you. I believe in you and I am cheering you on through this process.

I want you to pay close attention now.

It is important that you understand that your past, your mistakes, your perceived failures, and your pain have not been for nothing. I want to tell you that it was all preparing you for your greatness to start emerging now. There is no mistake that you are here, and there is no mistake that you are reading these words.

This is your time now. Have a seat and relax for a moment.

Your soul, the inner depths of the real you, is starting to step forward. And this is scary because your true worth does not rest on somebody else's shoulders. It is not from what other people think. It is not the money you make. And more importantly, it is not from the tricks that your mind has played on you while attempting to make you feel small and insignificant. I want to tell you that there is a greatness so powerful within you, that you may not even be able to imagine the amount of power you truly possess.

Together we are going to open the door for it to start shining. However, we are not going to pull the door off at once, blinding you, as, frankly, it may scare you like it did me. We can do this together, just a little bit at a time. You are going to crack the door open and take a little peek inside. Once you start getting used to your true radiance and who you truly are, then we are going to slowly open it just a bit more. *This is a process.* Sometimes it will seem like you are going backwards. Other times it will seem like you are sliding to the right or to the left. But I promise that you are making progress and you will continue to make progress. The trick is to know that you are making the smallest of steps, even when you feel nothing is happening. You are in the center of a huge whirlwind and it is moving all around you. The center of this whirlwind will start to bring you to a place of calm and inner peace. You will start to feel more relaxed if you choose to open to this process.

First, you need to make the decision that you want that door open, because once it is open, there is no turning back. You will become limitless! It will take time. And it could be that the life you have now may change for your highest and greater good. Sometimes this looks like chaos. Other times it seems like hardly anything changes, except what you feel inside. So, I need to know: "Are you really ready for this?" You are still reading this, so I know you are ready to receive the keys to start opening this door. Next, I will discuss how you can set yourself up for success.

Notes:

Chapter 2

SETTING YOURSELF
UP FOR SUCCESS

To continue to access your greatness, there are a few important things you need to understand. Accessing your greatness will lead to tapping into your intuition, which will directly activate your true inner magic. This is what makes you magnetic to draw to you aspects of your dream life and will provide you with the ability to have more happiness, love, freedom and wealth. When you are free inside, you experience more joy than you could ever imagine.

Have you been working endlessly, but you have not reaped any of the rewards that you feel you should have? The reasons and excuses that many people use, were created from all the suffering, pain, and misery which resulted from the belief that you are not good enough on some level or another. You may have been programmed to believe you have to work hard for what you want.

You may have believed other people's opinions, and they were faulty ones at that. Understand that these other people have been subjected to the faulty opinions of others, and, therefore, they have become opinionated themselves. It seems natural because society has agreed to it on many levels. To get to the truth of your being, there are techniques that will allow you to start expanding your inner greatness, and you will start uncovering your personal truth.

This truth is that you are worthy beyond measure,
and that you are beyond compare. You are valuable,
precious and rare. There is none other uniquely like you.

SUCCESS CHANT WITH ARCHANGELS

To increase your odds of success, you can use the power of Archangels.

If you are new to calling on Archangels, I will guide you through.

First do an internet search for an angel of (name what you are looking for help on). In this chapter, I did a search for angel of success. There was many that showed up, but I resonated most with what was mentioned about Archangel Sachael. This angel works with streams of success, brings wealth, prosperity and helps with harvests as well as harmony and material gain. The planet this Archangel's is associated with is Jupiter. I love Jupiter as it is the planet of expansion. Jupiter energy inspires us to take risks, to grow, expand and evolve.

After you discover which Angel or Archangel you want to work with, you then prepare a space to call this angel in and place your request. Know that you are not here to do all of this alone. The universe is on your side and wants you to be successful.

You can choose to use candles, incense or nothing at all. It's up to you as to what you feel is right for what you are asking for.

You pronounce Archangel Sachael as SAH-CHEE-EL.

I like to invoke them when I am in a relaxed state and have meditated for a bit prior. You can follow the following instructions. You can modify the following or you can create your own all together. The more creative you are, the better results you usually get.

I start to softly chant the Archangel's Name three times:

Archangel Sachael

Archangel Sachael

Archangel Sachael

I call upon thee and request thy presence.

I ask for your assistance or the assistance of a being of love and light to help me in all of my affairs. I am requesting that in all of my undertakings henceforth that you protect me and guide me to the right people, places, circumstances, and opportunities for my success.

I ask that you give me clarity of mind, clearing away all beliefs that hinder me from success. I ask that you wrap me in your powerful light and illuminate my path so I know what is the next step, next right action and the next right opportunity for me to accept. Warn me of going in the wrong direction in a fashion that I understand. Help me to the pinnacle of success.

I thank thee for thy presence. I thank thee for thy help. It is now done. It is now so in totally satisfying, harmonious, and perfect ways under grace for the best good of all concerned.

Please go about your business and let me know when you are near so I will pay attention.

Understand that you were never meant to have a small or insignificant life and you certainly were never meant to do this all alone. A lot of your emotional misery comes from believing you have noone or nothing you can rely on and not accepting support and help from others, including angels or by magic. Please understand that you are meant for great things in your own right. If you are not completely certain of who you truly are, there is hope. For now, consider your authentic self went into hiding for a while.

You did this because, when you were a child, you learned that only certain behaviors were rewarded while others were condemned. You may have been the wonderful little girl or good little boy who loved being in the spotlight. It was cute at first, but as you grew older, the rules began to change. You didn't know why. What was cute before started to become annoying. Or what was fun prior was now too childish. And because you wanted the same attention you had prior, you may have been called selfish. You were anything but selfish, and this caused you to be confused. You no longer felt safe and, little by little, agreed you would never allow yourself to be hurt again. With each agreement you made with yourself as a child, a part of your hid away. At times, you may have felt you were struggling with the questions: "Who am I?" "What do I want in my life?" And now, when you look around, you may only see the great suffering in this world and feel hopeless about not being able to change anything.

It started coming together for me when I was coming apart. I was diagnosed with conditions someone in their seventies would usually experience. I was thirty-nine. I thought I was taking care of myself. But there were things outside of me that were demanding too much of my time and energy. I was the Chief Executive Director for a home health care facility for twenty years, which took a toll on my health, my life, and my relationships. I had to learn to make myself a priority to save my life. You may feel like you are running out of time and have to start making some changes now, before you have issues in your life. It is my desire to encourage you to avoid having to deal with any major life crises. Or maybe you have already experienced them. Either way, this book will be a guide for you to access your true greatness, while discovering the magnificence of your soul purpose in the process. This will lead you to having a life that is successful beyond your wildest dreams.

What are you feeling at this exact moment?

Write your thoughts down about what you feel your greatness might be either below or in your journal.

Next, write down what you feel success means to you. It's hard to know if you are successful if you don't define what that means for you.

When you want to have a successful life, it is extremely important that you make yourself a priority. This means using your internal reference point as a means to gauge where you are, compared to where you are going. It does not mean comparing yourself to some external reference person, place, or thing. It entails taking care of yourself first, before you take care of others. This allows you to take care of others from a base that is overflowing. I do understand that this might be one of the hardest things you can possibly do. It was one of the hardest things I learned in my life. Once you get used to it, it becomes one of the most rewarding things you can do. It is something no one can ever take away from you. You may be saying: "I get that, but I do not know where to start or what to do!?" Take my hand and let us go on a short journey.

In your journal, write down all the ways you currently take care of yourself. It can be as simple as sleeping, eating, and brushing your teeth. Next, write down how you take care of your emotional self.

Do you give yourself permission to be silly at times?

Did you draw, paint, dance or do other things when you were younger that brought you joy, but you no longer schedule time in your life for these things?

What is the one thing you can start doing once every other week, even if it is only for 15 minutes?

Start investing in yourself and give yourself permission to take the quiet time you need to regroup and energize. Remember that from this space, you can start overflowing in goodness. You then use this overflow to care for your career, family, clients, business, and so on. If you are saying: "I know this," but are countering it with: "I do not have the time" or some other excuse, stop for a moment. How would your beloved feel if you kept telling them that? If you are making excuses for why you cannot take some time for yourself, please look at why. Look deeper inside and start to unravel where you first learned that it is not alright to care for yourself first. This may even be somewhere in your body. Ask your body where you are storing this and then ask it how can you let it go. If it is not in your body, ask your soul self if it is in your lineage somewhere. Don't worry if you can not find this stored in your body. I may be in your energy field.

To start the process of dissolving these energies;

Envision a beautiful light of any color you desire that flowing from the top of your head to the tips of your toes. This beautiful light is now dissolving the darkness that has been blocking you. If you need a visual aide, light a candle and imagine this being burned away as the wax is melted.

If you would like to get more creative and ask for the help from Archangels, you can call on Archangel Uriel and/or Azrael. Both of these Archangels will help with dissolving these issues and add powerful emotional healing.

If you really do not know how to take care of yourself, then think of how would you treat a celebrity or honored guest who was visiting you. Treat yourself in that manner. Self-care does not have to be expensive. It can be more precious to take a half day for yourself and go for a walk at a local park. Start acting as if you, yourself, are the cherished love that you have always wanted. If you are working with your inner child, start by providing a safe haven for him or her. Have fun! Go get your favorite ice cream or any other favorite treat!

I love buying myself fresh fruits and vegetables from local farmers. If your life is anything like mine, you have probably been told that you are different, do not quite fit in, and do not act normal. That is okay, because you really are completely unique, valuable, precious, and rare. You were never meant to be like the others. Leaders rarely are like the others. *It's the very differences that you are that make you great!* It is what legends and legacies are made of. You are rising above the rest who prefer to have a mediocre life.

You can begin with treasuring your body. Focus on the attributes that you do like about your body, even if you just like your eyebrows or your fingers or one piece of yourself. Just start somewhere. If you truly want to have high self-esteem and you want to like your body, ignore the insanity that is on television. Avoid the marketing propaganda that they put out there trying to make you feel bad. A lot of the marketing is specifically made to make you feel like you are missing out on something, you are not good enough and "this product, item, or whatever it is" will make you look better, become smarter, remove this or hide that. Before you know it, you have become a shopaholic and feel worse now than before, plus now since "you deserve it all - all at once" you may have racked up some pretty nice credit card bills.

If at all possible, know that magazines use photo modifications to make pictures look flawless. Television uses special lenses and cameras to make the images more appealing, etc. To make matters worse, our society is set up to compare ourselves to each other. It makes us feel like it is me against you. And this system has also downplayed our unique talents, skills, spiritual gifts and personal contribution we bring to the world. We are tricked into believing this is good, yet that is bad. If you work in this job, then you are bad. If you work in that job, then you are a good. It's all a trick to deflate your confidence and make you look outside of yourself a gauge of what your faults are. Get rid of these lies you believe. If you are doing the best you can with what skills, education and knowing you have - then you are doing what needs to be done. Don't let others take your light away from you. Shine so bright you blind the lies and your illuminate the world.

Taking care of yourself gives you the passion, energy, and desire to help others from an abundant source, rather than from an exhausted point where you feel you have to do everything for everybody. You are valuable, precious, and rare. Only you can provide the unique spark that nobody else has. Radiate your light, and your life will start flowing.

Notes:

Notes:

Chapter 3
THE B WORD!

Once you start taking time for yourself, you will also notice that you will have to start looking at the big bad "B" word. Now I do not mean "that" B word. I mean Boundaries.

Have you ever felt bad about using the big bad B word? That is, have you felt bad when you had to start Setting Boundaries? The B word, as some call it, can be a rough one for many of us because we do not want to be perceived as mean, cruel, evil, or selfish. Oh yeah! The big "S" word, "Selfish," that is sometimes sneered at us by manipulative people. There will be words or tones of voice underhandedly used against you when others cannot get their way, in order to take advantage of your money, time or energy. All because you used the Big Bad B! It is best to allow your Boundaries to become your big brother! You set Boundaries to protect yourself and allow you to have a healthy relationship with yourself and others. Let me tell you, as a recovering doormat, this is not an especially easy one for me. It seems that, as soon as you set a new boundary, people suddenly start trying to cross that boundary. You get hit with it left, right, and sideways.

After setting boundaries regarding no longer giving away my money, I was hired for an undesired job at a call center within 3 weeks. The strange thing was that I did not apply for this position. I was sent to the site from an accounting temporary agency I applied for several months prior. My mistake was accepting that position, thinking that I should accept any opportunity that came to me, because it would bring in more money. Wrong! It was not that bad an experience personally, but being terminated after five days of training was very uncomfortable. I talked to my self-worth boundary and decided what I was willing to and not willing to do for money. Needless to say, it really made me feel worthless for a bit. I knew I had a lot more work to do inside of me. I forgot to look at this from a larger perspective of my soul and ask myself: "How does this help me and my soul's agenda?"

I started having people ask if they could borrow money for medical problems, or because they were overspending, or so they could pay their rent. I got another wake-up call when I picked up the tab when going out to dinner with other people. Oh, my gosh! It was as if everybody and their brother knew that I was not to give away my money anymore, so they had to test my new boundary!

This is a test from the Universe, because it really wants to know if that is what you really want. Are you serious about setting that boundary? How does it make you feel when you have somebody cross that boundary or you "have" to be nice? How do you handle the individual that goes off on you when you say: "I am sorry but I cannot do that for you right now.?"

When you are setting boundaries, your deepest fears may come up, and you will be tested one way or another. How do you handle this? How do you get through this? Many of us agonize over this again and again, every time a boundary is set.

I found a simple solution, which I call: the "won-mirror-exercise." At first, I thought this to be almost too simple in my mind. I put my hand over my heart and I tapped 3 times using the same hand. I say out loud, staring at myself in the mirror: "I pledge allegiance to myself." After I say this 3 times, then I say: "So shall it be." The frequency of doing this is up to you, and depends on how much work you need to do with a particular boundary.

You start your own-mirror-exercise, by taking a deep breath and asking yourself three times: "How would not standing in my truth affect me?" Once you know how not standing in your truth will affect you, you will be able to start setting better boundaries. After you set a boundary, you may still feel uncomfortable with stating "No" to others. Understanding why "NO" has such a bad rap helps you learn how using NO saves you from future endless suffering.

Remember when you were younger and you had the phenomenal idea that you just wanted to touch something? Remember your parent's response? Whenever you wanted to grab something, you heard in a shrill voice: "NO!"

That kind of shocked you the first couple times, did it not? After a while, you learned what a YES was and what a NO was. You began to associate the word YES with things that you could have, while identifying the word NO with things you could not have, were not good for you, or were possibly dangerous.

First it was things that were dangerous, such as: touching a hot stove or putting your forks in an outlet. This progressed to: do not eat this or do not wear that. Then, you started saying No to yourself, even when your parents were not around.

When your parents asked you to do something, if replied with No, most of us were reprimanded for not agreeing with or not doing whatever was requested. This eventually turned into feeling unworthy and inadequate if you did not fulfill somebody's request. This has left you feeling lonely and powerless. You hear a lot of people tell you that it is okay to say No now that you are an adult. But you still have that uneasy feeling inside of you that you are doing something wrong. This is especially true if you are saying No to somebody you admire, love or respect. Now, whenever you say No, you start getting those feelings you had when you were a child. Maybe you experience a gut-wrenching feeling inside when somebody asks you to do something you do not want to do. If you are unsure about wanting to do something, instead of saying No right away, you can lessen this feeling by asking questions about what is it they want from you. An example would be: "How much time is it going take?" If you are busy at the time they ask you to do something, you can say: "Would you ask me again later this evening when I am not busy so I can look at my calendar?" This will give you time to think about whether or not you really want to do it.

In the meantime, you can start practicing saying No with a friend or a loved one who will help you. The only way you can start managing your own personal life is by allowing yourself to know and accept when you are stretching yourself too thin and are not able to help other people.

Sometimes it gets easier to say No to certain people, but it is still very difficult saying No to others. This is OKAY! It is also alright to stop beating yourself up because you just could not say No to that one person. This is an excellent time to look at how you feel about that person. Delve deeper into yourself to figure out why you feel compelled to say Yes most of the time. Let us get to the root of the fear that is holding you back from claiming your personal power. Does this other person make you feel insufficient? Do you feel like you are a servant to them? Maybe you feel this person has authority and you might get into trouble if you say No. Regardless of how you feel, instead of just yelling No, ask this person questions, so you can understand exactly what it is they want from you. And, if you need to tell them: "Let me think about that.," it is alright. If the person says that they need an immediate answer ("right this minute"), or it does not look like they will take No for an answer, they may be intentionally manipulating you.

People who manipulate are emotionally and mentally toxic for many women who are generous, compassionate, and kind hearted. It is best to eliminate as many toxic people from your life as possible, so you are not put in situations where you feel that gut-wrenching sense of guilt, because you said No or were not able to comply with their request.

When you are able to honor yourself from the inside, set boundaries, and take back your personal power, the people that have been toxic to you in the past will start to slowly slip away.

Do not let boundaries stop you from achieving greatness. Here is a positive affirmation to overcome this problem:

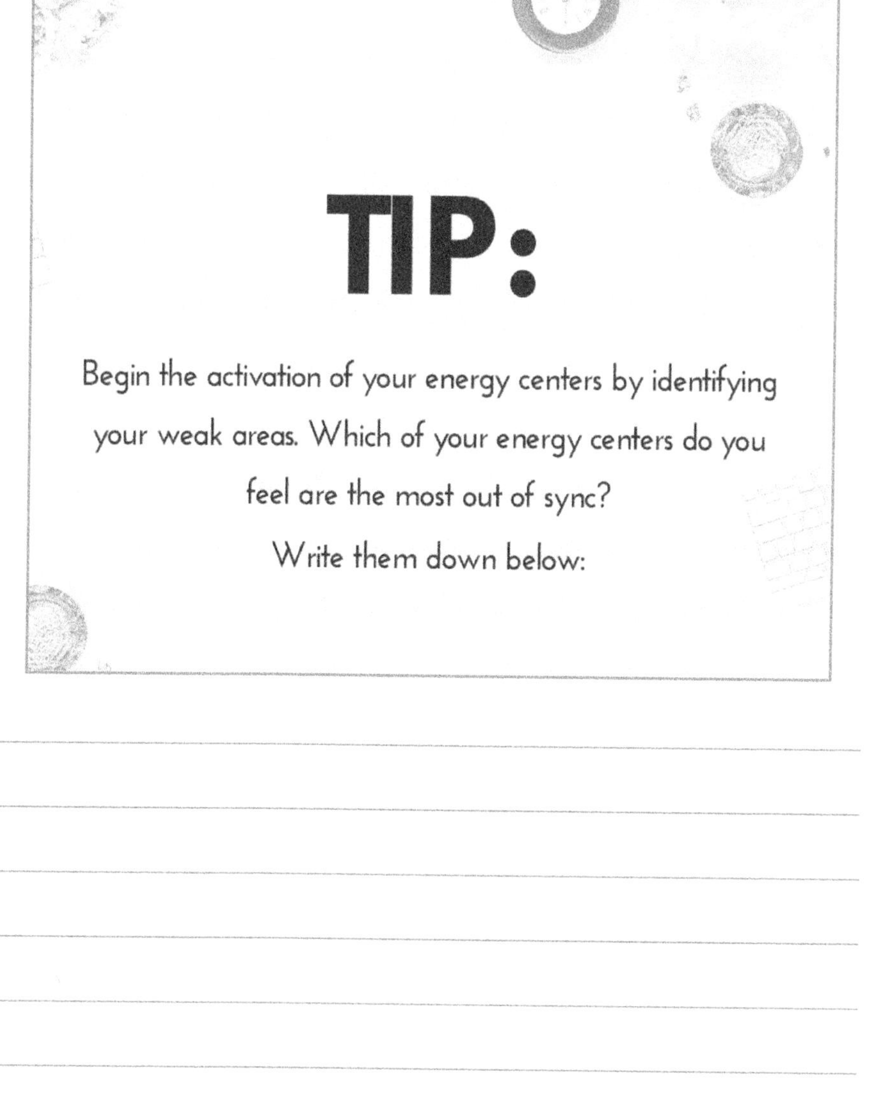

Why You May Have Had Weak Boundaries in the Past

To understand how you have come to view your body and your life as undesirable, you have to understand where part of it, if not all of it, comes from. I would like to talk about the television and other forms of marketing propaganda. Propaganda is biased and has a leading point of view intentionally designed to make you feel guilty and ugly. It is meant to manipulate you into feeling this way, so that you act in a certain way. Usually, these attempts are to manipulate you into purchasing their products or using their particular service.

Not all marketing and propaganda is bad. There are honest marketers and others that truly provide you with excellent brands and services to enhance your quality of life. Understanding the different forms of marketing empowers you to make better decisions for yourself. Understanding how these tactics play with your psychological makeup allow you to see how they affect your choices and decisions.

The first form is usually Testimonials. These are people who have used the products or services and have had good results. The key to understanding testimonials is that the results are unusual forms of success. Not just average success, but extremely unusual success. You have to look at how many people are claiming this. Then determine if you feel you would benefit from these products or services.

Another form is called "Framing." Framing is used to tell a story that presents only the good points of a product or service, to influence people into taking the desired action. It also points out the bad consequences of not taking that action. This can be used by those trying to manipulate you as well. It takes you back to setting good boundaries and seeing the bigger picture before making a decision.

"Bandwagon" is for a party or a movement attempting to get mass appeal, where the sheer number of its followers is used to move it forward. One of the most successful bandwagon advertisement campaigns was a female with her arm up as if she is flexing a muscle with the words saying: "You can do it."

These forms of marketing or propaganda leave you confused as to whether their product would really be best for you. The first thing you need to do is stop and ask yourself questions. Ask yourself:

"What do I know about this product or topic?" Do an internet search. Ask yourself: "Just because it is popular, does it mean it is good or right for me?" Ask whether this really fulfills your needs and whether you feel the price is truly worth the product or service. Keep this in mind when you are creating boundaries and setting yourself up for success.

To keep you moving forward and help you get closer to your personal road of riches, there is something very important to understand. You need to understand that we live in a vibrational world and things that appear solid are actually billions of tiny microscopic atoms buzzing along. Science is finally starting to discover more about what mystics and other wise people of ancient times have been saying.

In the next chapter, I will give you a very brief understanding of how vibration works and how you can use it to benefit you.

Notes:

Chapter 4

How Vibrational Energy Works

In the mid-1990s, I was introduced to a concept called Quantum Physics. I did not fully understand what it meant at first. This led me to dig deeper into the truth of how this world works. We have preconceived ideas about how this Universe functions. Many have heard about the Law of Attraction and tried to make it work, but were not able to fully create what they wanted. That is because they do not understand that everything is vibration.

Scientists started to discover vibration in the mid 1830s. The invention of the Electron Microscope in 1931 made testing their observations possible. Today we are able to see movements in common everyday items, including ones that we do not normally think of as things that are actually moving, such as paper, wood, plastics, etc. Without getting into all the scientific details, I will explain how this works, and why you need to understand it enough, so you can start manifesting money, freedom, joy, and the life you truly desire.

We are all familiar with a guitar and strings of a guitar. Each time you strum on a string of a guitar, it makes a sound. This sound is like putting a drop in water. It vibrates outwards into the world. Sometimes the sound is beautiful; other times it sounds awful. Some people can hear a melody and think it is the most wonderful thing in the world, because it resonates with them. At the same time, another person can listen to the exact same melody and think it is terrible and does not sound right at all. It triggers an unexpected emotional response. It really sets this person off. They become intensely irritated and hate it, while not fully understanding why. They become increasingly frustrated simply because they heard this particular piece of music. You might be asking yourself: "How does this relate to creating more money, having more freedom, and experiencing more joy?" I am really glad you thought about that. Let me explain.

Everything we see, touch, feel, read, or hear are echoes of a vibration. What you are currently reading or listening to is the vibration of my thoughts, and I use words to imprint them on this paper. If you close your eyes and allow yourself to really "feel these words," you will be able to feel the deep love I have for awakening your greater self, flowing from my heart to your heart. Each of us is made up of atoms that vibrate at a certain speed. Even items that appear solid are tiny atoms vibrating at a speed that allows us to perceive them as a solid object. This vibration causes a very minute song that is only measurable by the most sensitive of instruments or seen with high-powered electron microscopes.

Sometimes the vibrations cause harmony and other times disruption. I would like to talk about a very important key that may be difficult to understand at first, but it will be easy to sense if you pay attention.

Vibrations can cause emotional disharmony also. This can lead to an *emotional trigger* that you may not have previously been aware of. One of the goals of discovering emotional triggers is to disarm them so they will no longer affect you in a negative manner. To explore this more in depth, I will discuss how you can identify an emotional trigger.

An emotional trigger can be set off for seemingly no apparent reason that you are consciously aware of. You could be doing something, or someone, and they say something that does not sit well with you. You may start to experience a range of feelings that do not make sense to you.

When you start feeling different types of emotions, there is something going on that needs investigating. You sense something, but may not be able to place your finger on it.

In this case, let us say you read something that sets you off. You feel an instant anger that stems from your belly upwards. You feel that, whatever it is, is wrong, bad, horrible, or any other word you would like to label it as. You feel angry and frustrated. You feel helpless or ready to do something about it right this minute. From this point, it starts to replay in your mind and you think of ways for you to solve this, fix this or get rid of this.

Many times, it is our greatest emotional suffering that leads us to desire to make this world a better place. It strengthens us to have the endurance to accomplish great things, have mass influence, and to change the world forever. If you are still reading this, you have this inner strength which is needed to start transforming your world. You also have the strength to start transforming your outer world and create a ripple effect on a global level.

Your inner emotional turmoil can lead you to want to do things you have never done. My inner turmoil has led me to take a stand to empower women to have more money, more freedom, and more joy in their lives. I have become relentless in my pursuit to educate women on how to manifest millions. I know empowered women will have more choices, better healthcare, more influence, and, therefore, become unstoppable. Women that have money will find ways to make this world a better place.

Look at your inner emotional, physical or other abuses or misuses of power that have been used against you.

Can you find the silver lining where this has allowed you to gain the inner strength to accomplish whatever you set your mind to? Stop for a moment and write down some areas where you were able to use the pain and suffering you've experienced to make a change in your life. You can use your journal to write these down.

Perhaps you have it in your heart to help others in some way or fashion. If you had a business that created six, seven or eight figures a year, how would this change the way you help others?

Exercise: Grab your journal or notebook and your favorite writing tool.

Using paper that you will be discarding, write down everything that has made you so angry that you could not bear it. You do not have to use words. You can use scribbles, symbols or signs. As you work, it is important that you put your inner rage into this page. Give yourself permission to use words you normally would not use. Swear if you desire to. Get stomping mad and keep writing until you can no longer write, and you feel all that frustration going straight into the paper. Keep writing it all out. If you have to get up and pace back and forth, stomp around, point your finger, yell, scream or jump up and down, then do so. Just let this emotional feeling consume you and then go back to writing it out. Once you have done something physical, you may notice that you feel a bit calmer and more relaxed.

Now that you have written all this out, find a fire proof bucket, clay pot or use an outdoor fire pit, grill or other place where you can safely start a fire.

WARNING: Do not do this inside the house unless you have a fully functional fireplace, a clean chimney and you've opened the flue.

Set the paper on fire and, as the smoke rises, imagine all the pain is removed with it. Imagine that all the suffering is burned away and the root cause is now dissolved. It is rare that you will need to do this a second time. However, if in a few days, you have the same emotional triggering, do this exercise again. This time consider writing down not only the circumstances, but also what you would do if you could go back in time and change what occurred. Then imagine taking your younger self out of the chaos and placing her in a safe zone where you can care for her personally. Once your younger self feels safe, imagine some type of water element, such as going swimming or a soft warm rain, washing away the pain and purifying your current and your younger self. Once this purification happens, you can bring your younger self into your heart and begin to merge her incredible talents and gifts into your current world. This is not to be used in lieu of professional help. If you have had a traumatic childhood, consider finding a professional that specializes in inner child work and integration. Another factor to look at when you are desiring to create more wealth in your life or to have the life that you dream of is to look at how your energy system affects your ability to manifest. This energy system is commonly referred to as the "chakra system." This is not even a close estimate of the full explanations on the chakras. This brief overview will give you some good insights.

This science and discipline has been practiced for many centuries. What initially emerged in the Indian Subcontinent (from Hinduism) as a concept of internal balance in an ancient book called "Vedas," is still practiced to this date.

Initially, it was thought that there were only 7 chakras. However, with our evolution most individuals have 12 of chakras activated and they simply need some attention and alignment. In the next chapter, I will discuss a basic overview of the 12-chakra system. I will tell you a bit on how you can balance each one and what you will gain by doing so.

Notes:

Chapter 5
THE CHAKRA SYSTEMS

Chakra has various interpretations of the definitions as well as functions of chakra, since people are recently more aware of the significance of chakras and how they play a role in balancing the physical, mental and spiritual state.

However, chakras can be simply explained as the energy centers that exist within our bodies. Its name originated from an old Sanskrit word that means "wheel," "circle" and "cycle"- which describes the spinning motions of Prana (vital life force energy) at these points.

These energy points serve as openings for Prana to flow through our physical bodies, where it will be taken up and collected to be transformed and emitted for use. These energy centers correspond exactly to the seven main nerve ganglia and are responsible for regulating physiological processes like the immune response, organ functions as well as psychological processes such as our emotions and behavior.

On the physical body, there are seven major chakras present in the body. The three lower chakras (Root Chakra, Sacral Chakra, Solar Plexus Chakra) are associated with core emotions and needs, as the energy circulated at this particular area vibrates at a lower frequency and is denser in nature.

Meanwhile, the four upper chakras (Heart Chakra, Throat Chakra, Third

Eye Chakra and the Crown Chakra) correspond to our higher mental and spiritual aspirations. The remaining five Chakras are outside of the body and connect you to greater levels of spirituality and connectedness. In order to be stable on an emotion, mental and physical level, people have been practicing chakra balancing for centuries. It's fascinating how the concept managed to survive throughout the centuries. Something which was followed for ages and is still ingrained in cultures around the world must be effective and must show promising results.

The different chakras each have a specific color associated to it, which can be attributed to its energetic existence. The frequency of the vibrations it emits results in the different colors that are characteristic of the different chakras; this can be explained by the manifestation of the different colors we see, which is essentially the vibration of electromagnetic waves emitted by light at different frequencies. In chakra healing exercises, which will be given later, color plays an important role.

Each chakra point is equivalent to a specific aspect of human behavior and development; the balanced flow of energy at these different energy points ensures that the body functions smoothly.

However, a blockage or unbalanced flow of energy in any one of these energy points will result in the manifestation of health and/or emotional and behavioral problems. This leads to the inability to lead an abundant life, as issues in one part will often have overreaching consequences on the other parts of your life.

The main intention in discovering our chakras is to learn how to master each chakra's essence and unite them all in a balanced energy field. When we are able to identify the different energy fields and balance them out accordingly, this will in turn reunite all our detached inner elements to a higher conscious of self-awareness.

HOW YOUR CHAKRAS CAN HELP YOU?

Our Chakras are basically energy systems, which have the power to connect our mental state to our physical state- both playing a pivotal role in maintaining a healthy and happy life. The thing about first seven Chakras is that they are located in the physical body, giving them the ability to impact our physical health. However, this also makes them capable of controlling our mental state as well. For example, the First or Root Chakra is located at the base of the spine, and is normally also what keeps us grounded- thus affecting how secure and supported you feel in life. Your Chakras can help you in numerous ways:

Affecting your physical health

As your Chakras have a physical connection to your body, and not just a spiritual one, it only makes sense for them to affect your body's functions as well. For example, the Root Chakra which has been mentioned above, when unbalanced can lead to back pain and fatigue. Your Heart Chakra, located in your chest can affect your heart, along with the breast, blood pressure and immune system.

While awareness regarding our personal energy and the importance of managing it has increased, we still tend to give more importance to our physical health- as compared to our mental health. In line with such practices, keeping your Chakras balanced is surely something which everyone should look into.

Affecting your mental health

While taking care of your physical health is quite important, there's no denying the fact that your mental health deserves the same attention. Fortunately, your Chakras can really aid you in this process. Other than helping us feel secure, something which the Root Chakra does, our Chakras help us in numerous other ways, such as ensuring we feel confidence, helping us communicate well with others, learning to love and enjoy new experiences and many more important functions.

Keeping all these aspects of your life balanced basically leads to a state of peace and contentment, something which every human aspires to achieve. However, our Chakras can easily become imbalanced- especially when negative energy surrounds us and we don't have the chance or time to listen to our own mind. Keeping your chakras balanced is the key to achieving a state of well-being, and fortunately, with all the attention Chakras are getting now, finding the right guidance is no huge task.

Each chakra represents a certain part of our bodies as well as consciousness or behavior. A disruption in balance in any one of these chakras will have an impact on either our health or emotional and behavioral states - which will indirectly impact the state of abundance in our lives. This also includes abundance in terms of our finances.

A person's ability to manifest money in life would be affected significantly, as well as their attitudes towards money. For example, an imbalance in a certain chakra would result in a person's low self confidence, which is crucial when it comes to making decisions and pursuing opportunities.

This will then end up with the person not being able to earn more money in life to live the kind of life that they want.

Hence, I will go more in depth of the seven major types of chakra and their specific characteristics, as well as the psychological and physiological aspects that it corresponds to. We will also look into how an imbalance in any of these chakras can affect us financially. Later, with regard to each chakra problem, we will also suggest practical steps as well as exercises you can take to realign your chakras, ensuring that you achieve abundance financially, as well as in all other aspects of your life.

By going beyond our 7 basic chakras and seeking to activate and align your 12 Chakras, you can open the portal between the Worldly and the Divine. You can awaken and manifest the abundance the Universe is offering you. With the awakening of the new energies on Earth, there are different ideas about what color and sometimes the actual location of the eighth to the twelfth chakras.

BASICS OF THE CHAKRA SYSTEM

1. The Root Chakra/Muladhara (The 1st Chakra)

This chakra is located at the area between the genitals and anus, which is known as the perineum. It is represented by the color red - owing to the fact that it vibrates at a lower frequency.

The Root Chakra is all about being physically there and having a sense of belonging in any given situation. It also corresponds to your survival instincts where it gravitates into a point of trust and self-preservation.

If this chakra is active and balanced, you feel grounded, stable and secure. You don't find it hard to put your trust in people. You will feel present in your current being and feel connected and rooted to your physical body. However, when this chakra is weak and not activated, you may feel inferior in terms of your appearance where this can be your weight, height or body shape. You may also feel that you're not pretty enough and you do not have direct control of your life. You feel that you're not good enough and can easily feel unwelcome when it is not the case. Therefore, you are in a constant battle of fear and tension.

It is also possible for your Root Chakra to be overactive. If this is the case, you are easily agitated by the slightest provocation. You might also be someone who is materialistic and be overcome by greed. This may result into addiction of different sorts.

For instance compulsive gamblers, drug addicts, alcoholics, video-game addicts as well as shopaholics. These are all results of an overly active Root Chakra. When you've become comfortable in that state, it is hard for you to revert back and change for the better.

This particular scenario can be observed with teenagers nowadays who are rebellious and are caught up in social ills as a result of wanting to prove their point and identity crisis. This happens when they do not have a sense of self, and are willing to do anything because of peer pressure to feel more worthy of themselves.

Your Root Chakra is also known as your Money Chakra. The following questions will help you know if your base chakra is out of balance.

Do you have bouts of feeling anxiety, stress or guilt over money? Is it difficult to handle your finances well? Or is it hard to accumulate material wealth?

These issues may very likely be caused by blockages or imbalances in the Root Chakra which usually manifests itself in the form of fear and major insecurities about survival - this ties in closely to financial security, as our basic needs in life are dependent on this aspect.

With an unbalanced root chakra, you will constantly feel insecure when it comes to your finances, even if your income is a sizeable amount. Your survival energy is centered on money, and every bill or expense that comes your way makes you feel behind. You have an unhealthy obsession with money and feel the constant need to keep finding ways to earn more money, and feel stressed when you don't.

You may also find yourself in a less than ideal career, and face financial problems all the time. You may feel stuck and sluggish, but yet your fear holds you back. You never feel like you are good enough and this affects your drive to achieve what you want in life. These are all signs of an imbalance in the Root Chakra.

With a balanced Root Chakra however, you find yourself more confident in yourself as well as your ability to earn and manage your finances. You organize your finances well; you have enough for what you need and want in life. You are also more unlikely to have an unhealthy preoccupation with money or material things.

If you find yourself facing the same issues I spoke about earlier, do not fear - for a solution to your worries is here!

Ground Yourself

Stop whatever you are doing and step into your garden (or the park), without your shoes; the idea is to be close to the earth beneath your feet. You can choose to lay down on the ground, or walk around in the dirt/grass barefooted. Another good way to do this also to visualize roots extending from your feet to the centre of the earth.

Physical Exercise

Exercise of any form and kind is also an effective way to help with an unbalanced Root Chakra, whether it is yoga, jogging, football or just a simple walk - just get up and moving! Doing this will help activate stagnant root chakra energy within you.

Incorporate More Reds In Your Life

It can be your clothes, your house or the items you use. Since red is the colour of this particular chakra, engaging with the colour red will certainly help to balance this chakra.

Meditation

Seek out a quiet, comfortable place and sit or lie down. Begin to visualize a glowing deep red light emanating from your Root Chakra, and feel the pulsation of its warm radiance. Watch (in your head) the light become a glowing sphere, and imagine a red four petaled lotus flower unfold - you may realize that you have trouble getting the sphere to spin or the flower to unfold itself, which is a sign of blockage. Keep breathing intent and energy into the chakra until the sphere can spin easily and freely. Proceed to send the energy of abundance throughout your entire body through the other chakras.

Foods

What you eat is what you are - this theory also holds true here. Consuming root vegetables as well as naturally red colored foods such as meat, apples, beets and other root vegetables will certainly help balance out this chakra.

2. The Sacral Chakra/Svadhisthana (The 2nd Chakra)

The Sacral Chakra is located slightly below the navel, exactly four fingers down from our belly button. It is represented by the color orange. This chakra corresponds to our emotional and sexual desires as well as our ego.

When the Sacral Chakra is active and balanced, your feelings flow freely and you are not over-emotional in expressing them. You are open to intimacy and you are passionate. You are full of life and people love being around you as you bring very positive energy. Most importantly, you do not have any problems in expressing your sexuality.

However, if you have very low Sacral Chakra it is hard for you to enjoy and live in the moment as well as appreciating life. You tend to be stiff and unemotional and you always have your guard up.

For example, when someone throws you a surprise birthday party, you feel indifferent or you do not know how to react. Ideally, you should be happy and thankful for the thoughts of others of you. Instead, it's hard for you to receive and open up.

On the other hand when the chakra is hyperactive, you tend to be overly emotional and over-reacting to even the most trivial things.

People do not usually like to be around you as you are very unpredictable and it is possible for you to explode at any given time.

When both overly active Root Chakra and Sacral Chakra combine, it is extremely hard for you to accept rejection and you become too overly attached to other people, especially when it comes to romantic relationships.

For instance when your boyfriend or girlfriend choose to break up there is a high chance for you to injure yourself or do something out of the ordinary that is going to cause you harm. You think irrationally or you may not think at all when proceeding with a certain decision.

Ask yourself these questions to discover how the Sacral Chakra may be affecting your money:

Do you get sad or angry at the notion of money? Or are creative (or anywhere close to good) ideas hard to come by?

This signals an imbalance or blockage in the Sacral Chakra, which is where we process our emotions around money (being the chakra centre that is responsible for our passions, desires as well as emotions).

A blockage right here also blocks the flow of creativity, as the Sacral Chakra is the place where creative energy is processed and converted into physical things. Since creativity plays a major role in the manifestation of money, this becomes a hindrance when it comes to making money.

When the Sacral Chakra is balanced, you will naturally be able to seek out the opportunities available in the world around you - since your flow of creativity is unrestrained. Not only that, money will no longer trigger negative emotions in you.

Again, if you are currently experiencing symptoms, it's not the end of the world - help is on the way. To address a blocked or imbalanced Sacral Chakra, you can try these activities to regulate this particular chakra center.

Shake Your Hips

Yup, you got that right. Go on and gyrate those hips! Latin or African dances or any other movement that involve shaking your hips are great ways to activate this chakra. Hula hooping is also a good activity to do this. I like to do the Egyptian side step and the figure 8 with my hips to loosen them up and get my creativity flowing. While you are doing this, imagine the seat of your soul sitting in your hips. Most individuals that I have worked with that want to be spiritual have the seat of their soul in their heart Chakra. When your soul is seated properly, it will help sustain and rejuvenate your body.

Water Related Activities

Water is the Sacral Chakra's element, so it's only natural that being close to or in water will restore balance to this chakra. Relaxing near or wading in open water sources such as rivers, lakes or the ocean is a good activity to balance your chakra. Taking warm relaxing baths or a shower is also one good way to recharge this chakra center. Even listening to sounds of flowing water can help calm and release the energy flow.

Make Your Life More Orange

It can be your clothing, or the items you own; surrounding yourself with orange things can help to stimulate and bring balance to the Sacral Chakra.

Meditation

Again, like all other chakras, meditation is a practice that helps greatly (which is why you should incorporate it in your daily life routine!). Visualize an orange lotus or crescent moon at the area of the Sacral Chakra (slightly below the navel), and breathe deeply while keeping the image in your mind for a few minutes.

Foods

Eat foods with orange colors such as pumpkin, papaya, and oranges. Use spices such as cinnamon and these will help activate and rebalance the Sacral Chakra. Drinking a lot of water will help too.

3. Solar Plexus Chakra/Manipura (The 3rd Chakra)

This chakra is located at the center of the body, specifically at our stomach level. This is where the physical energy is distributed. It is represented by the color yellow and has a higher vibration frequency as compared to the Sacral Chakra.

The Solar Plexus Chakra corresponds to your feelings when you are in a group of people. It is responsible for the development of relationships of all kinds, such as a romantic relationship, camaraderie or with your family members.

This chakra also represents your individuality, self-esteem and how you stand up for what you believe in in the presence of others. It is the center for unrefined emotions as well as personal power.

This is where we develop a sense of self and an outward sense of others. With the mastery of this chakra, you are able to directly perceive the feelings of others as well.

When this chakra is inactive, you have very low self-esteem and it's hard for you to acknowledge your self-worth. You feel useless and powerless especially when you are under pressure. This result in you saying "Yes" to even things you do not believe in.

Let's illustrate an example. Let's say you are assigned a project with your colleague. For the project, you came up with all the ideas and did most of the work. When you have presented the project to your boss and it was well received, your boss asks who came up with the concept and your colleague takes all the credit.

You really want to speak up and tell the truth but you do not know how. You are afraid that conflict may arise between you and your partner, so you just keep quiet. In the end, your boss offers your partner a promotion and because of your unwillingness to stand up and speak up for yourself, you missed a golden opportunity. As a result, you feel depressed and disappointed and it adds more to your feeling of unworthiness. Therefore, the cycle never ends.

On the other hand, if your Solar Plexus Chakra is overactive then you can become a very dominating person and would want to control everything. Your personality can be likened to that of a dictator. In the workforce context, you will be perceived as a very stubborn and controlling leader. It is likely that your subordinates will feel pressured and stressed when working under your supervision.

The Solar Plexus Chakra also corresponds to your financial condition. When your chakra is balanced and active, then you will easily become a money magnet. If you own your own business, it is easy for you to attract customers as well as closing deals.

However when your chakra is inactive, you will face financial crisis such as finding it hard to earn money and also saving money!

If you answer yes to the following questions:

Do you find that you have to put in an extreme amount of effort and hard work in order to earn money? Or do you have low self esteem and lack the drive to get what you want?

Your Solar Plexus Chakra may be blocked or imbalanced.

This chakra is known as the "money center" - it is where people either get absolutely rich, or falter and fail.

This chakra plays an important role when it comes to personal power – it creates action. A blockage or imbalance in this particular chakra will manifest in the form of low self confidence - which is crucial when it comes to making decisions and taking advantage of opportunities that come your way, and help you manifest money.

When this particular energy center is balanced, you will see a marked improvement in your finances. Not only that you will feel more confident and possess the willpower and drive to take action and make decisions.

You will have the ability to manifest what you want - and this includes money.

If the symptoms above perfectly describe your current situation, you can use the methods below to restore balance to your Solar Plexus Chakra.

Soak In The Sun

Since the Solar Plexus Chakra is represented by fire, it is only logical that being in the sun has tremendous chakra healing powers. Go outdoors in the afternoon sun - perhaps take a short walk.

Stop The Victim Mentality

Knowing that you are not "powerless" helps greatly with blockage in the Solar Plexus Chakra. It takes a lot of energy to play the victim, and maintain that façade, and not only that, it removes us from the weight of self-responsibility. Explore what it feels like to say no, and step up to claim responsibility and power over your life.

Let Go Of Unhealthy Attachments

Unhealthy attachments are a massive source of energy loss, as well as a cause for Solar Plexus Chakra blockage and energy stagnation. Ask yourself if said object/belief/memory/desire doing yourself any good and acknowledge it is, then let go - take care of yourself.

Make A Change In Your Daily Routine

Break out of routine, step out of your comfort zone and start trying out new things- it doesn't have to be a major change; even small breaks in routine are helpful. It can be just opting to wake up a little earlier in the morning to do some light reading or exercising before heading off to work, or it could be even arranging to meet with friends for dinner for a change instead of eating alone on weekdays.

By sticking to "safe" routines, you will only serve to sustain feelings of powerlessness within you. By stepping up your routine, you will not rely so much in your natural source of confidence and the energy of self belief, but instead be forced to get out there and be yourself and to also focus on action. This will help grow your confidence levels in leaps and bounds.

Stop Associating With Negative And Critical People

Cut off (or at the very least, keep them at an arm's length away from you) such people who criticize and belittle you from your life, as they will only be a deadweight to you during this time. Instead, only surround yourself with people who will support you and help you grow, and know that you have the power within you - it's entirely up to you to decide on the people who will stay or leave in your life.

Give Yourself Some TLC - Tender Loving Care

Make an effort to take care of yourself every single day, psychologically as well as physically. Identify areas in your physical, mental, emotional or spiritual health that you have been neglecting, and be sure to address that issue head on. A healthy level of self-esteem is essential for a balanced Solar Plexus Chakra, so take care of yourself - it's a form of self-respect and self-love too.

Laugh

The greatest source of strength and power within all of us out there is being able to find humor in the most unlikely moments in life, especially during our darkest and lowest moments. Freedom is found in finding humor in life, so laugh at yourself. Lighten up and don't take life so seriously - you'll only disconnect yourself from your source of power.

Foods

Complex carbohydrates like whole grains such as rice and rye are good to balance out the Solar Plexus Chakra - foods like this provide a sustained supply of energy.

Spices such as turmeric and ginger are good energy sources too; they provide a heating element to your body. Not only that, naturally yellow foods such as bananas, corn and pineapples are great to consume; they help balance out this energy center too.

Surround Yourself In Yellow

Wear yellow clothing, keep yellow decorations around the house - these practices will help you with your chakra.

Meditation

Focus on the area where your Solar Plexus Chakra resides (the upper abdomen), and visualize a glowing yellow sphere. Slowly concentrate on making it bigger while it rotates; that area will feel warmer and more relaxed. Do these for a few minutes, then let the energy dissipate and take a few breaths, after which you should open your eyes.

4. The Heart Chakra/Anahata (the 4th Chakra)

The heart chakra is located at the center of the chest, or specifically at the heart. This chakra is both green and pink because it relates to inner and outer love. It vibrates at a higher frequency in comparison with the Solar Plexus Chakra. The Heart Chakra corresponds to love, kindness, spiritual growth, compassion and devotion. It is the bridge connecting the higher and lower energies of our being. It balances your emotions.

When your Heart Chakra is balanced, you are compassionate and kind where you will be committed to maintain harmonious relationships with others. In contrast, when it is under-active, you are distant with the people around you where you will be cold and mean to them.

For instance, you do not like intimacy and you refuse to help those in need as you feel burdened. You will refuse to aid anyone without further consideration.

When the Heart Chakra is hyperactive, you tend to become a foolish person and your excessive love for others may suffocate and cause pressure to them. You do not know boundaries and you will want to love others your way.

For example, in the context of a romantic relationship. If your Heart Chakra is too active, you tend to control your boyfriend/girlfriend's activity and whereabouts each and every day. This no doubt invades their own personal space and time where it shows how you overthink things and controlling every single move that they make.

One obvious indication that your Heart Chakra might be over-active is when your pulse races unusually fast, in stressful situations.

When it concerns the Heart Chakra, there can be two extremes and sometimes too much of anything is not always good. For instance, yes you have to be compassionate to others but that does not mean you should say "yes" to each and every person who deems your help.

On the contrary, some people may not care at all or have compassion for others. Needless to say, they will completely ignore others if they are in need of help, regardless if it's a friend or a stranger. Therefore, it is important for your Heart Chakra to be balanced or it will result in two extreme conditions.

In the context of money or financial situations, the heart chakra plays a significant role in shaping how you feel about money. It also corresponds to the feeling of worthiness in attaining the money.

Firstly, when the heart chakra is blocked or inactive, you will feel that money is hard to achieve. There is also a tendency to feel that money is the root of evil where it may lead to negative consequences in your life.

This can be greed, ungratefulness as well as selfishness. When you feel money is hard to achieve, you can't seem to find any possible solution to make money happen, where in reality there is an infinite number of possible ways to make your financial situation better. Therefore, how you feel will indirectly influence how the universe reacts towards you.

You may also feel that money is the root of all evil, where people who are rich or are born with a silver spoon in their mouths are all greedy and selfish. Therefore, you do not want to be associated with money.

However, if your heart chakra is balanced and active, you feel that money is a powerful medium to achieve and manifest your goals in life. It acts as a tool for you to do what you love and to fulfill your soul mission. For instance, if you love traveling the world, then money can make it happen for you. You achieve a stable financial status and it will also be easy for you to attract money as well as the amount you want in order to do what you love.

There are several solutions you can take in order to activate and balance your heart chakra. Firstly, is through different activities:

Meditation

Sit down in a quiet and comfortable place, and close your eyes. Take a couple of deep breaths to calm you down. Place both of your palms on your heart. Imagine a beautiful green flower opening from a tight bud to full bloom.

As your mind visualizes this, in the context of your money chakra, feel the energy of appreciation for money and see it flowing in yourself. Then, weave a figure 8, which is an infinity sign using your fingers, repeatedly in front of you as you think of this thought in your head; I am always experiencing money flowing in than flowing out. I can now use money in pursuing what I love. Then, bring your palms to the center of your heart and feel the energy within you. Take a deep breath and open your eyes when you are ready.

Schedule A Regular Time To Do What You Love

Commit to doing what you love. This can be your passion projects or your hobbies such as baking, volunteering or hiking. Set a schedule to make sure you adhere to the time and you make time for it no matter how busy you are.

Follow Your Dreams And Desires

Do not let your dreams die just because you do not have time to realize them. Make time and work on them consistently. This can be having that dream house or it can even be building a business you have always wanted.

Foods

As stated in the previous, chakras are all connected to specific energies within yourself. Therefore, you may select certain food that contains specific vibrations or energies which may help balance your chakras.

As the heart chakra is represented by the color green and pink consider eating green leafy vegetables, pink grapefruit also known as ruby red grapefruit, mixed greens, salads, and other green vegetables can help in balancing the energies. This may include kale, any form of lettuce, spinach, bok choy, broccoli and other green vegetables.

The heart chakra is all about balance and green veggies are neither yin nor yang in traditional medicine. Therefore, they maintain a perfect equilibrium that is essential to this chakra.

Self Love Rituals

Creating rituals with the direct intent of learning more about loving and caring for yourself will also help open and balance your heart chakra.

I like to create a fun ritual where I take a long bath in herbs and essential oils, dry off and put on something that makes me feel absolutely wonderful. I put on some soft music, light white candle and then write down and affirm how wonderful I am.

I am Wonderful, Valuable, Precious and Rare; there is no other uniquely like me

I am a Treasured Being and gracefully accept the best of care and richest fare that life has to serve me

I open myself and empower myself with the knowledge, wisdom and knowingness of each step to take towards fulfilling my divine purpose while living an abundant and joyful life

This, or something better, now manifests for me in totally satisfying and harmonious ways for the highest good of all concerned

As I will so shall it be

I thank thee

I thank thee

I thank thee

The longer combined version I created is:

I open myself to my Life Purpose and Path

I love myself through and through for there is no other uniquely like me

I am valuable, precious and rare. I validate myself

I communicate with clarity and compassion for I fearlessly speak my Truth with Love and Compassion

I express myself and my greatest potential

I am divinely inspired and guided

I acknowledge myself and choose to act in my own best interest

I call forth the truth of my being

I am valuable and worthy

I reclaim my truest self and my Personal Power

I bring forth my essence

I am precious and I am rare

I expand from deep within me - my true self

I love myself through and through

I love myself from deep within for all that I am

I bring forward my ancient sacred self

I accentuate my unique I AM presence

I draw forward my divine immortal self with ease and with grace

My divinity shines through my heart and through my divine

I illuminate my true essence

I am beautiful

I am powerful

I am light and

I am bright

I call forth my infinite sacred self

I enhance and empower myself from every point

I enhance my Charismatic influence

I attune myself to the infinite abundance of the Universe

I empower myself and I speak the universal truth for the best good of all concerned

I open to my greatest and highest gifts

I open to my highest potential and my highest good

I open to receive that which is mine by divine right and Divine Selection

I open to my own good

And

I open to receive the luxury that life has to offer me

I open to receive gifts, money, wealth, compliments, love, affection, warmth, health, beauty, homes, vehicles, jewelry, flowers, my divine selection perfect mate, and riches

I now activate my blessing powers to help others open to their greatest and highest good

I now open and am ready to receive that which is mine by divine right and divinp selection

I call forth the seeds of success to sprout and to bloom

I call forth my Glory & Grace to be act activated

To create an orchard of good, wealth, health, beauty, and riches in my life

I pledge allegiance to myself for that which I AM with honor and integrity

This, or something better now manifest for me in totally satisfying and harmonious ways under grace for the highest good of all concerned

It is now so

It is now done

I deeply and profoundly Love Myself and I make my life Worth It!

I thank thee! I thank thee! I thank thee!

I am so grateful"

Creating your own self love ritual is the can be far more powerful as you are using your personal creativity and making it your own. You can also use the ones that I have created too. The combined one I created activates the second, third and fourth chakras.

5. The Throat Chakra/Vishuddha (the 5th Chakra)

The Throat Chakra is located at the throat and is represented by a light blue color. It vibrates at a higher frequency as compared to the Heart Chakra.

The Throat Chakra is mainly the center for conversation, self-expression and creativity. This is where your inner voice or your own truth is expressed. This chakra also corresponds to diplomacy, your relationship with others as well as detachment.

When your Throat Chakra is balanced and active, you willingly express yourself and are not restricted to do so. However, when it is inactive, you tend to shy away from expressing yourself as well as your creativity. This often leads to untapped talent and not unleashing your true potential.

For instance, you are required to attend a meeting. During the discussion, your boss asks for everyone's opinion on whether the office should open up a new branch at a different state. Most of your colleagues do not favor the idea as some of them would need to be transferred to the new branch.

But for you, you think it is an excellent opportunity to grow the business and learn new things. However because you are too afraid to express your thoughts and how you really feel, your boss dismisses the idea.

Many people have the idea that people who have a very inactive Throat Chakra are only the shy and introverted types. This is not true. Inactivity of the Throat Chakra can also be associated with those who speak up and are fluent in their speeches, but they rarely speak the truth. Therefore, the inactivity of the Throat Chakra can be understood in two perspectives; firstly referring to those who are unable to express themselves and secondly, those who do not speak the truth.

What happens when you have a hyperactive Throat Chakra? You tend to have too much to share and control the conversation in a negative way. It can also cause you to not think before you speak and sometimes your words may come across as offensive to others. As a result, people will try and avoid you as you are not a good listener.

In the context of money or financial situations, the throat chakra plays a significant role in speaking your truth and worth. There are many ways that a blocked throat chakra can manifest its way to money challenges.

Firstly, a blocked throat chakra will stop you from communicating what you deserve or speaking your truth. For instance, you are uncomfortable in asking your manager for a salary raise that you really deserve.

This also applies in the context of lending money to other people. You may be afraid to ask the person to pay back the money they borrowed from you. You are not honoring yourself by speaking up.

There are also circumstances where you will need financial assistance but you are too afraid to do so and you think too much of what others may think of you. This happens when your throat chakra is blocked and you are afraid to confess on your money mistakes.

However, when your throat chakra is balanced and active, you are able to communicate your worth and problems in regards to money. You will ask for your deserved raise, the money people owe you as well as not afraid to talk about the financial problems you are facing. You are not afraid to speak your truth and recognize your worth.

What to do when your throat is out of balance:

There are several solutions you can take in order to activate and balance your throat chakra. Firstly, is through different activities:

Sing Whenever And Wherever You Feel Comfortable. You can sing in the car, when you are doing your laundry, in the shower or wherever you feel like it.

Be Open And Honest With Those Around You

Speak the truth with as much compassion as possible. You don't have to be brutal with the truth. Do not trade your authenticity for the sake of approval of others. Be yourself and it is important to be genuine in everything you do.

Learn To Say 'No' Kindly And Firmly

If you find yourself in a situation where people are forcing you to do things against your principles, you have to learn how to say "No." It is hard sometimes to do especially with people who are close to you but if you say yes all the time, you are compromising what your own truth and standards.

Foods

There are several foods and drinks you can consume in order to balance your throat chakra. As the color blue represents this chakra, blue foods, such as blueberries will encourage expression. Coconut water, herbal teas, and raw honey helps also.

Fruits work well to balance this chakra, specifically fruits that grow on trees such as lemons, apples, pears, peaches, apricots and plums. The reason being is symbolically these fruits are said to be true to themselves. They only fall off the tree when they are ready and ripe.

6. The Third Eye Chakra/Ajna (the 6th Chakra)

The Third Eye Chakra is located between the eyebrows. The chakra is represented by the color indigo. The energy vibrates at a higher frequency than the Throat Chakra.

The Third Eye Chakra is the center of intuition and direct spiritual vision. It is through this chakra that we are able to visualize things through our "third eye" of intuitive knowledge. This chakra also represents forgiveness and compassion.

When you have an actively balanced Third Eye Chakra, it corresponds with your spiritual awakening. You also tend to have good intuition and you dare to achieve your goals.

We usually associate people who have good intuition of having the "sixth sense." These people will usually give you advice on certain issues. For example, they may say you should not trust a person or work with them as he or she is trying to take advantage of you. It turns out that their advice was really worth taking as the incident really came true.

When you ask these people on how they developed their "sixth sense" ability, they themselves are also unable to answer. The question is, how and why do they have this kind of ability? This is because they have a more balanced and active Third Eye Chakra.

If your Third Eye Chakra is inactive, you tend to depend on authority rather than instinct to make your own decisions. You may also have deluded thoughts. This also results in you being too dependent on conventional beliefs rather than rational.

People with a very weak Third Eye Chakra are also very weak in visualizing and organizing their lives. For instance, if you were to ask them how they see themselves in a matter of 5 years, it is highly unlikely that they can answer this question as they are unable to visualize their future.

People with a weak Third Eye Chakra also have this mindset that it is unnecessary to have future plans and too think far ahead. Usually, these people will have a negative perspective of life.

However, when your chakra is overactive you may live in your own world and you always over think. In extreme cases, this may lead to hallucinations where you create problems that were not even there in the first place.

How your third eye affects your money:

When your third eye chakra is blocked, it will be hard for you to visualize yourself owning more money. You are also unable to foresee what you are able to do with the money you have; which includes helping others in need.

The most common reason for this blockage is because you always see the world through other people's opinions as well as beliefs. You are easily influenced by other people's outlook.

For instance, some people may have a perception that money and wealth will only shape you into a greedy and selfish person. When your third eye chakra is blocked, this is when you believe each and everything that people tell you without rationalizing.

As a result, you stay away from money as well as having a bad perception towards people working towards it. This will only create confusion because it is not your truth.

When you have a healthy third eye chakra in regards to money, you will be able to mentally visualize the opportunities that money brings to you. You are able to spend it wisely by achieving your dreams, helping those in need, and donating more to charity.

There are several solutions you can take in order to activate and balance your third eye chakra. Firstly, is through different activities:

Listen More Carefully And Attentively When You Are Engaged In A Conversation

When you engage in a conversation, ensure you take the time to listen attentively as there may be hidden messages, which may shape or influence your truth.

Try engaging with the energy of those around you

Try and feel the energy around you, are they emitting a positive or negative energy? And if so, why? Understand the reasons.

Praise and credit yourself for your correct intuitions

Always trust your intuition, especially in making decisions. When you are right, credit yourself for it. This means you are in tune with your third eye chakra and you know your truth.

Foods

There are several foods you can consume to balance and activate your third eye chakra. As the chakra is represented by the color indigo, fruits such as blackberries, plums and grapes are effective in balancing your hormones and intuitions. You may also consume purple yams as well as purple cabbage.

7. The Crown Chakra/Sahasrara (the 7th Chakra)

The Crown Chakra is located at the top of the head. It is represented by the color purple and is vibrating at a higher frequency as compared to the Third Eye Chakra. It is also the energy with the highest frequency vibration among the 7 major chakras.

The Crown Chakra represents the highest level of consciousness, knowledge and wisdom as well as your sense of the world as a whole. It is the connective center to your spiritual being. This chakra integrates all the seven chakras of your body with their respective qualities and characteristics.

When you have an actively balanced Crown Chakra, you have full awareness of your emotional as well as a spiritual being. You are also aware of the world and its existence. You are not prejudice and you are an excellent learner, as you love to regard your experiences as new lessons in life. Therefore, you are able to pick up new lessons effortlessly.

However, if your chakra is inactive it is quite hard for you to acknowledge and be aware of the spiritual world. You also have a hard time picking up new things. Another indicator is that you are unable to think clearly when you are under stress or pressure.

When your Crown Chakra is hyperactive, you tend to overthink a lot. You can't let things go easily and you create problems in your head that were not there in the first place. You are over-enthusiastic in chasing the spiritual world that you neglect what your physical body needs.

As the Crown Chakra is associated with knowledge and wisdom, many people disregard the fact that there needs to be a balance in whatever they pursue. Thirst for knowledge and learning new things are positive things to adopt but when it becomes extreme it may become the direct opposite.

Let me give you an example. When a person has an overactive Crown Chakra, he or she has this undying thirst for knowledge that they are willing to fly to any country to learn new lessons. They will travel from one country to the next while disregarding the fact that it incurs a lot of cost. The situation worsens if they pay their expenses using credit cards and each and every time they choose to travel, they add more to their debt.

Another example is because you want to achieve an inner balance of your spiritual being you meditate for 24 hours even though your body is already exhausted and you have not eaten.

This will cause your health to deteriorate and it will not help you to achieve your inner peace in the long run. Therefore, whatever it is that you choose to do always remember striking a balance is key!

When your crown chakra is blocked, you constantly feel the need to seek approval from others in making any money moves. You are easily affected by other people's perception towards you.

For instance, some people may say that money is the root of all evil, you will be easily influenced by this and this will affect your pursuit of making money in creating the life you want.

Not only that, when your crown chakra is imbalanced, you will be a slave to money. You are not in control of your money. Instead, it has control of you. You are overcome by greed and you feel that you can't live without money.

When you have a healthy crown chakra, you have a self-realization that you have permission to create as much money as you like, spend it the way you want. You acknowledge that you are not your money and you have control over it. What other people may say about money does not affect you.

What to do when your crown is off balance:

There are several solutions you can take in order to activate and balance your crown chakra. Firstly, is through different activities:

Practice Meditation within reason

Meditation gives you great calming effects. It also enhances your focus and helps you achieve positive energy flow. Practice meditation daily for only 10 minutes and you will see a big difference in yourself. Try to control your breathing as this will help you to think better and calm you down.

Read Inspirational Books On A Daily Basis

Grab an inspirational book and try reading one chapter per day. The book can be from a public figure you adore, or anyone you can relate to. This will not only help to inspire you, but it will also widen your horizons.

Include Some Peace And Quiet Into Your Daily Routine

Sometimes you get too overwhelmed with your hectic life and all you need is some time for yourself. Find a quiet place, go to your favorite coffee shop or your favorite park and unwind. You need to have a balance in your life.

The Herbs To Balance Your Chakra

There are several herbs you can use to help balance your crown chakra. However, do note that these herbs are only to be ritually inhaled and not consumed. These herbs are sage, juniper, copal, frankincense and myrrh.

Before I move onto the higher chakras, I wanted to ask you if you are often beside yourself? What I mean is does your heart go in one direction and your mind goes in the other direction? I know mine use to do this all of the time. I always heard "Follow Your Heart" - but my mind would cause all kinds of roadblocks or I would rationalize why that would be a bad decision. It was gut wrenching every time it happened. I felt like I was in a tug of war with my heart and what I thought.

Then, I discovered a way to fully stop this vicious cycle and it was such a relief!

Can you imagine being congruent with your heart and mind so you can speak your truth with love and compassion?

Do you know how much more powerful you become by doing this one simple thing?

Remember, that you booked marked the ** Mind and Heart in Agreement Exercise ** because it is one of my deepest secrets on how I was able to become in alignment and stop betraying myself!

For the eighth to the twelfth I will be giving you less information than the first seven because you have to have the first seven working optimally to have these one activated and aligned.

8. The Soul Star Chakra (the 8th Chakra)

The eighth Chakra is located two to twelve inches from the top of your head. It is represented by the color black and deals with the karma from the past. It is the gateway to your higher self and is considered to be your Soul Star Chakra. It is the link between you and the higher consciousness and the Divine. When this energy center is active, you are able to experience a spiritual connection with divinity, the higher powers. This connection allows the divine light from above to enter your earthly being and to nourish and energize you. The eighth chakra is also your spiritual "GPS" - meaning when you are in alignment and balanced with this chakra you will know your next step. The hardest part is when your next step is to be present and not to "do" anything. As you are in alignment and balanced with this chakra, the negative patterns of your past starts to dissolve and are replaced with your soul's guidance.

You can tell this chakra is blocked when you are unable to let go of situations and can not forgive. Other symptoms include you feeling guilty when someone accuses you or others of something that you did not do.

Some of the ways you can work on this chakra is to work on knowing you did the best you could with the knowledge, experience and limited negative patterns that you were stuck in and start doing whatever rituals, prayers or others to forgive yourself.

Always start with forgiving yourself and accepting responsibility for your part and at the same time have more compassion for yourself. As you become more and more forgiving of yourself and others, you will go from a life of misfortunate fate to a life you were destined to live. Your destined life is always full funded by the universe and even though you have some tough times, you always know what you need to do next.

9. The Spirit Chakra (the 9th Chakra)

The Ninth Chakra is located approximately eighteen inches or about an arm's length from the top of your head and it allows you to connect your spirit to the divine source. The color its associated with is Gold and helps you understand your soul purpose and unity with others. It would connect you directly with the Source of all things and allow you to communicate with ethereal beings from around the galaxy, angels, and stars. Once this divine gateway and connection is activated, you will become increasingly aware of your hidden spiritual gifts.

This Chakra also holds the beliefs about universal love and what needs to be done regarding care for yourself, others and globally. When you are fully in alignment with this Chakra you start to express your caring and kindness for others in everyday life. You start to lose an internal loneliness and it's replaced with a beginning sense of being cared for by the universe while you start to feel a connection with the living energy of all that is. From this perception, you are able to start seeing the true spiritual truths and it assists with integrating your spirit with your body. You start to act out your spiritual truths and take action steps without having doubts.

As you focus on being connected to this Chakra, focus on having your truths revealed to you. Write them down. Focus on unconditional love for yourself and allow this Chakra instill its intelligence within you.

10. The Universal Chakra (the 10th Chakra)

Your 10th Chakra is located above the ninth and is also connected to the earth. This chakra is sometimes called the Earth Star as it deals with your relationships to the environment - meaning it is related to the people, places and things. Earth tones affect this chakra. The tenth chakra is also considered the Universal one, connects you with the Universe and aligns your physical self with your divine body and light. It helps you connect and feel a sense of oneness with the Creator as well as all His other creations. This is the chakra that draws the natural world to you and brings circumstances into your life. You are able to enhance this chakra by being in nature and noticing how you interact with things of nature. When fully connected you will know which herbs or natural healing work would be for your healing. When you have this chakra activated and aligned it will reflect how well you live as a physical human being and helps heal your ancestry and help you transcend the body and travel in the Universe. To have this chakra fully functional you need to balance your masculine and feminine energies. At this point you will start experiencing a life with less effort and more in alignment with your soul's destiny. Once fully actualized this chakra turns from earth tones to a pearlized color that illuminates.

11. The Galactic Chakra (the 11th Chakra)

Your 11th Chakra, the galactic one, connects you to the galaxy and is a pinkish orange color and is above the 10th as surrounds your body. This chakra corresponds with the solar plexus and allows you to diminish the past, present and future tramas that have been stored in your third. This chakra helps balance the inner and outer personal powers that allows you to call your personal power back when it has been taken or you've given it away either intentionally or unintentionally. When this chakra is activated, you are able to transcend through the bounds of time and space are able to travel in the galaxy through teleporting and being able to be at two locations at the same time and manifest things from the virtual to the physical realm. You are able to find the attachments to misperceptions you have and heal the issues stuck in your tissues. In essence, this chakra transmutes negative to positive, heals trama's, family patterns and issues.

12. The Divine Gateway Chakra (the 12th Chakra)

Your 12th Chakra is a shimmering clear golden color and is above your eleventh chakra that transcends downward and surrounds your entire energy field. It is the link between the Divine Gateway that connects you to the other worlds in the Universe and the galaxy and the realms of collective consciousness. It is about seeking oneness with the omnipotent and omniscient Creator and all of creation through ascending. This chakra allows you to tap into the Golden Christ Healing Energy which is transformational and helps you connect with all energetic forms of life.

The best way to keep this and the other upper chakras activated aligned and functional is by creating some form of spiritual discipline that works for you. For me, I like to focus on taking time out for myself to meditate. I ask for help from my guides and guardians and source directly. Once a year I go to a place for a silent retreat and focus on being washed clean by spirit. Usually on a daily basis I use the eject button to get rid of thoughts that I do not want to create in my life. I will talk more about the eject button in the ten keys to success.

The Importance of the Chakra System

You have now understood the location and function of each chakra. Now, let us look at the broader picture and see how this system can help you in life:

It Helps You Become More Grounded

You begin to realize the true beauty of life and the universe itself when you become more grounded with the Earth, when you become humbler, and when you have a better understanding of the reality. The root chakra can help you with that. It also benefits the kidneys, adrenal glands, colon, legs, and bones.

It Enhances Your Creativity

Your balanced chakras can enhance your creativity significantly. A balanced sacral chakra can help you control and channel your personal energy and help you. Moreover, it directly affects your physical, mental and emotional well being. You can use your renewaling energy that your chakras are providing you with to remove obstacles, create manifestations, renew and rejuvenate.

It Can Make You Braver

In this life, an optimal amount of courage is necessary to face the relentless ups and downs. Those who believe in themselves and have higher self-esteem are usually the ones who are the most successful. Your solar plexus chakra can provide you with the much-needed boost of self-confidence and courage to overcome the obstacles of life. This chakra aids in the healing and strengthening of the stomach, adrenal glands, gallbladder, liver, and muscles.

It Provides You with Peace

Every struggle that you are facing, every pain that you are enduring, every foe that you are fighting, and everything that you are doing…everything is part of a pursuit for peace. Inner Peace is the one thing which every single being is after. Fortunately, there is a center of peace within every human being – the heart chakra. Located in the chest, it's what keeps the heart pumping in a healthy way and your immune system in good shape.

It Helps You See the Truth Clearly

Peace, harmony, and success all depend on the single element of communication. If you think about it, most workplace and personal conflicts begin with miscommunication. The purpose of the throat chakra is just that…to help us communicate and express our feelings more clearly and effectively and become aware of the truth. A balanced throat chakra benefits the thyroid, the throat, and the oral health.

It Can Increase Your Intuition

Those who have a strong connection with the spiritual realm have strong intuition. This means that they can guess or predict things without having to use conscious reasoning. Multiple chakras can help you in this regard, including the third eye chakra, the soul star chakra, the galactic chakra, and the divine gateway chakra.

It Makes Your Spirit Stronger

Human beings are sophisticated creations made up of the spirit and the physical body. These two parts are deeply connected with one another. If one is damaged, the other one can feel its effects as well. Because of that, having a strong spirit automatically means having a strong physical body, free from all sorts of diseases and pain. It is crucial for the crown and the spirit chakras to be perfectly balanced.

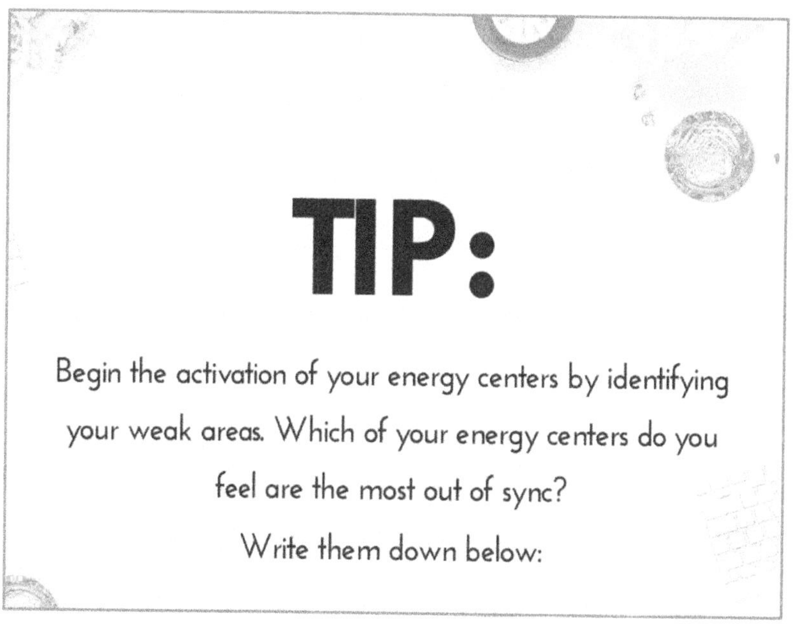

I hope that you are now equipped with the knowledge and awareness to work on your chakras. If you feel any physical or emotional disruptions and imbalances in your life, you should consider the possibility that they could be resulting from an unbalanced chakra. Please see a professional if you suspect something is wrong. All of the suggestions I give will enhance proper medical care. It's not meant as a replacement.

After working on your chakras and bringing them into balance, it is time to start digging into the ten keys to become more successful – The focus of the next chapter!

Notes:

Notes:

Chapter 6

THE TEN KEYS TO SUCCESS

Some of these keys may be new to you, and some may not. If they are not new to you, ask yourself if you are practicing them or how you could incorporate them into your lifestyle. Your circumstances will not change if you are unwilling to change. Open yourself to become flexible. You will get the most benefit from these ten keys if you keep an open mind and stay willing to explore potentials.

Key One:

The first key is to be honest with yourself and use it to recognize how and where you need to start stepping up your game. Being honest with yourself means that you are taking a good look at where you currently are, compared to where you desire to go. If you are unsure about where you desire to be, this key can be used as a great tool for determining that where you are is not where you desire to be. Think of ways that you can improve your life and in what areas.

Looking at where you are is a tool that you are using for self-improvement. This is not for you to use to make yourself feel small or beat yourself up. We all have come to a place in life where we have to look at exactly where we are, in order to know where we desire to go.

Using this key helps you accurately assess what you will need to do in order to start stepping up your game.

One way you can start stepping up your game is if you pay attention to your thoughts and use the eject button to remove thoughts that do not serve you and other people's thoughts.

Remember first there is thought, then word and then actions. So your thoughts directly affect what you say, how you respond with grace or ReAct with emotional outbursts and what actions you take or don't take.

Where's the eject button and how to use it to remove negative thoughts:

In my early 20's I discovered that there is an eject button for getting things out of your head that you don't want in there and this has truly helps me go fro a worrywart to feeling like life is going to turn out alright.

Your eject button is located below your third eye which is in the center of your forehead just between your eyebrows above the bridge of your nose. The way you use this and remove thoughts from your head is to use your pointer finger from your dominant hand and gently touch the spot where your eject button is located and imagine that your finger is wand that sucks the thought out of your head. You can state to yourself or out loud, "get out of my head." Or you can say, "Cancel, Clear, Delete." And you can come up with your own statement to get the thought out of your head. Be persistent as it may instantly reappear again until you start to get the root out.

If you have racing thoughts you can place your right hand over the right ear and your left hand over the left ear and command and demand your mind to "be silent." Keep doing these two exercises until you have a grip on your thoughts. You were never taught that you could much less how to control your mind. As a result there is more suffering at the hands of your own thoughts than ever before. Be kind to yourself. Be gentle on yourself especially when you are being truthful. You can have truth with compassion.

Key Two:

The second key is to start to grow rich in your thinking, and your pocketbook will be filled. You have the Power to choose your thinking. Beliefs are thoughts you continuously play over and over again in your mind. When your thoughts are of Prosperity, Wealth, Happiness, Joy, and Health, your world begins to shape itself around your new beliefs. So, have fun coming up with new ways you can grow Rich in your thinking. Make it a game. Ask others to join you and come out to play.

I have been practicing these secrets for over twenty years, and still have times when I need improvement. Just keep moving along and know that you will be able to make a huge shift in your life.

Key Three:

The third key is to step up your game by playing with the words you say and think on a consistent basis.

This might sound pretty easy. However, it is important to know that this alone will change your entire life, your relationships, and your finances. Have fun with your words; make rhymes and songs that make you laugh and feel good.

When you feel good and are playing with your words, you are activating the law of thinking.

Ridding yourself of negative words and thoughts will help you manifest happiness, wealth, and health. Remember: if you use your words like swords, they will slash yourself and others. Choose to use your words like a magical healing wand, and miracles and magic will follow you wherever you go! I will be covering exact techniques on how to do this process in the upcoming chapters. For now, you have a gateway, so you can start the transformation to begin manifesting the money, freedom, joy, and dreams you desire.

It is impossible to think of wealth and riches while you are worrying about poverty. None of us can think two different opposing things at the same time. Now, it is true that our thoughts may be so lightning fast, that as soon as you attempt to think of something positive, it immediately returns to your former status quo. You have a choice. You can choose one thought over another. First there is thought. Then there are words followed by actions. You can start by journaling and taking notice of your thoughts. Notice how they lead you to feel a certain way. Notice how tired and drained your body feels when you think negative thoughts, compared to when you think happier thoughts. Interesting, is it not?

You can choose thoughts that empower you and others. Or you can choose thoughts that disable you and slash others like swords. Choosing empowering thoughts, even while having a lot of negative ones, is the beginning of creating miracles and magic in your life.

This key will be the main foundation for you to open up to more prosperity in all areas of your life.

This key has formed the foundation to my prosperity and has contributed directly to my personal, financial, and business successes, as well as that of thousands of others I have taught and coached.

Key Four:

The fourth key is to ignite your imagination! Awaken your creativity, and you can imagine it is raining money in your life! Let it rain prosperity into your checkbooks and pocketbooks. Using your imagination will empower you to take inspired actions toward manifesting money, fulfilling your dreams, and living the kind of lifestyle that you desire. All this happens with more ease and grace. The struggles start to become smaller and smaller until they nearly disappear.

The trick is to envision it flowing to you like a river of abundance, without placing "rocks" in its way. The rocks are your attempts to control "how" the money comes to you and not being open to possibilities. As an example: many people believe the only way they can have money is by working for another person. Some believe the only way is to get more and more in debt with the hopes of someday getting that debt paid off. It is true that these are just two different ways of having more money, possessions or things in your life. But they are very narrow pathways, even if they have been generally accepted practices.

There are thousands of ways for money to fill your purse. You do not need to know "how" it fills your purse. Being open to follow your hunches and look for the signs, will allow more money to flow into your life.

Using your imagination and opening your mind to the possibilities is one of the most important keys you can use to unlock the barriers that prevent you from earning a consistent six figures or more per year.

Has it happened yet that you feel like there is nothing left for you to do now, as all has been tried and done?! Moreover, despite your constant struggle you simply have:

- No understanding of why you cannot seem to make more money.
- No understanding of why one crisis after another happens in your life.
- No understanding of how to overcome these issues and move forward.

Key Five:

The fifth key is to Unlock Your Super Powers by tapping into the power of your super subconscious mind. The real power is when you have accepted a thought or belief that benefits you to the extent that it is now programmed in your mind, for within the subconscious, all your reality is manifested without any effort on your part. The tricky part is knowing how to replace the beliefs in your subconscious that are plaguing you with bad luck! I will go more in depth about how our subconscious mind works in later chapters. These keys are preparing you to truly open up and ignite your passions.

Key Six:

The sixth key is to ignite your passions and set fire to your worth! You are a powerful being. By igniting your passions and allowing yourself to truly "feel" what it would be like to have your deepest desires manifested, you will generate a feeling of satisfaction and worth.

Just imagine a fresh ripe orange. Feel the texture in your hand as you circle its beautiful orange flesh with your finger tip. Imagine pushing your finger nail into its flesh and smelling the rich citrus scent. You can feel your mouth water and some hunger signals. It is absolutely delicious, is it not? Imagine biting into this fresh ripe orange and its flavorful juice bursting in your mouth. It is sweet and divine. You have a vivid imagination if you can taste it. If not, notice how your body is responding. This is an example of just how powerful your imagination really is. You have instant physical results that have been proven to you and thousands more throughout the years. This truly means you are a powerful being, and that you are worthy by simply being you.

Fuel your passions with your imagination and set fire to your feelings of worth!

Key Seven:

The seventh key is for you to open the door and receive your riches! You can do this figuratively or literally. Many of my clients have had the best results when they do this both ways. If you do not normally use your front door, go to it at least once a week to greet prosperity and welcome it in. You can welcome prosperity, divine love, abundance, money or whatever it is you desire to come into your home. Step aside and wave your hand as if you are showing an honored guest the way in. If you really would like to go all out, you can sing silly songs that you make up, open your front door, and welcome this quality in. You can even open the door, step aside, and wave your hand and state that you welcome it in.

This allows the Law of Prosperity to start working its magic into your life. When you are in agreement, you make the decision to allow the floodgates of wealth, riches, divine love, health, joy, and money to flow into your life. Remember to keep a journal and note successes as you watch your life magically start to change.

The point of this key is to raise your feelings of joy and happiness while taking action. If you are more into writing, drawing, hiking, biking, or some other form, use that. There is no right or wrong way you can do this. Some methods will work better for you than others. Some will work quicker than others. Whatever makes you "feel" rich and prosperous, do that more often. It is important to note that this needs to be done on a consistent basis. Sporadically doing this will give you random results.

These keys, I have discovered, have helped me go from a poverty mentality to an abundance mindset. The shift is not as hard as many think it is. Persistence is important, because you are developing a new way of life. When these become your natural habits, you are in the flow of life.

As children, before tramas and other upsets, they are naturally in the flow of life. As young ones, children state what is right in front of them. They are loud, they dance, make faces, state the obvious, and have huge dreams. Unfortunately, as you start growing up from a child into an adult, you start to be told not to dream too big or too much. Other times you may be labeled as "day dreamer." Well meaning adults, teachers, and others start to crush your dreams bit by bit. With this your self-worth is worn away and you are lead towards having a very low self-esteem. You are convinced that it is in your best interest and are often told, "so you do not get hurt" or "be disappointed." This is from their own training and narrow beliefs. Each generation trains the next. Though society has grown, evolved, and have become more aware in the last fifty years, there's more issues now. Ones our grandparents never realized. These new issues include being an empath, or some call it being too sensitive.

We are evolving into the true manifestors we were designed to become. With this we also have a great amount of new and interesting awakenings. You may have noticed you are, we are still not functioning at our full potential.

As adults, we start out with the world as our oyster and, as we get older, we start to shrink our dreams down to the size of our paychecks. You may have downsized your dreams instead of increasing your internal wealth meter. It breaks my heart when I think of all the creative women that have done this. This book is intended to create the changes necessary to restore your prosperity.

Key Eight:

The eighth key is to start following the road that is paved in gold for you. Meaning: start to dream a bigger dream than you had before. Start thinking of ways you would like your new fabulous life and finances to flow. You have the perfect opportunity to create a new life and to acquire the wealth to follow your dreams.

Infinite possibilities are opening up for you right now. All you have to do is follow the clues, hunches, and your intuition to be led to riches beyond your wildest dreams. This I know to be true, and I have never once regretted following my intuition. I have regretted not following it. I have questioned where my intuition was leading me. I even doubted I was following my intuition when I thought my life was going from bad to worse. I felt my future was bleak. It was only my perception. I did not know it was leading me out of my own darkness and not into the darkness.

As of today, start to expect the unexpected and celebrate that you are choosing to dream bigger and brighter than before. When the sails go in a different direction than you have planned, expand yourself rather than shrinking. When the economy takes a down turn according to the news and other people, it is time for you to seriously open your mind and ears and look for the opportunities. If you focus your awareness, you can see the problems others are experiencing and ways you can solve them. This is an opportunity. If you take action to inform them of the ways you can help solve their challenges, and charge a fee appropriate for the results, you will never be without money.

Have you ever met another person that is so full of life that they almost have a glow to them? Ever wonder what is up with that? Would you like to start glowing and manifesting like a billionaire? I know I did when I was first starting this journey. The secret to this is to choose to become that future person you are desiring to be. You do this by tapping into your own personal muse.

Key Nine:

The ninth key is to become tuned-in to your wealth vibes. This means you become aware that you have a money muse. That it is completely possible to become a money magnet, even if you have never been one before, or you were one but lost it in some manner. It is all a part of our lessons to be open to receiving and to be tuned-in to our own wealth. The goal is to understand the ebbs and flows of your wealth vibes. When you feel the twists and turns of your money flow, you can navigate better. You will make better decisions and notice subtle changes. To start noticing these changes, close your eyes and take in 5 deep breaths. As you feel the air coming in and out of your body, feel the energy around you. Identify what it feels like. As you breathe in and out, focus on your heart beat. If your mind keeps coming up with distractions, count the beats of your heart. Notice how the air flows from the top of your nose and from around your nostrils as it comes in, and how it seems to stream downward like a jet as it goes out. Notice that in this very moment, everything is wonderful. Focus even more into this very moment and, as you breathe, feel your body responding to your breath. Going deeper into your breath, feel how the hair on your body has sensations. Feel how the furniture is supporting you, and how you are able to let down your guard.

When you are fully present in the moment, you are able to realize that you are a powerful creative being. When you stay present in the moment, you are in your most powerful state. It is the gap between the thoughts what creates miracles and magic in your life. It is an oasis of all potentialities.

As you do this breathing exercise more often, you will become more alive, more tuned in, and turned on. This is the gateway to the infinite; an ocean of infinite wealth, potentials, divine love, freedom, and so much more... This space is where all the greatest ideas have come from; where you will be able to go, to create your sanctuary. This space leads you to make firm decisions and stick with them. In our last key, you make a decision to stay firm on creating your life on your terms, while living your dreams.

Key Ten:

The tenth key is to make the decision to accept dominion over your life, money, finances, relationships, how you feel, and your health. Prosperity is yours by divine right. Opulence is meant for all of us in this life. Make the call and give the command for abundant manifestation to flow into your life. It is your choice to command prosperity into your life; to receive and accept expected and unexpected gifts, or not. Having faith that it is already making its way to you, claiming it, and being grateful for it, will make it come to you quicker. This also means blessing the little things that take place; finding pennies, quarters, and dimes is a sign. Witnessing others near you experience prosperity, is a sign it is coming your way. You will notice how much abundance is truly awaiting you to receive it.

Even if at this moment your mind is telling you something different, correct your thoughts and restate what you desire to see in your life. Focusing your thoughts, energy, words, and actions all in one direction will bring what you desire into your life. If you are expecting to receive ten thousand dollars, it is already on its way. You will get little bits and chunks coming to you. If you continue to document and receive the small amounts with gratitude, it will flow in a rhythm. One of the biggest mistakes I see women make is assuming it will be here all at once. Another mistake is acting as if they will not be making any more money in the future. An attitude of: "Today, this is all I have, therefore, this is all I will ever have." Become mindful if your thoughts. Lead yourself into a mindset toward confidence in the future. Also, do not base your joy on outcomes like: "If I win the lottery, then I will be happy." The natural laws of prosperity do not work that way. That is the inverse of the law. If you are happy and a high emotional and vibrational match, you will receive the wealth you desire. The trick is to allow the flow of your wealth come from all directions. Meaning, you could find money as you are on errands or you may get an unexpected refund. Or you find missing or hidden money that you didn't know about. I have personally gone to state websites that list missing money that was turned into them and found several hundred dollars. I have also found money for my friends and family from insurance policies they had forgotten about or from deceased relatives they did not know had passed.

You get to choose where you want this to lead. Your imagination is the limit, and your imagination has no real limits. Look everywhere; leave no stone unturned. You are on a treasure hunt, and the Universe will leave you clues to where your fortunes lie.

Notes:

Chapter 7

WHY PROSPERITY SEEMS SO DIFFICULT TO ACHIEVE

We all want prosperity. We all desire it. But we have so much difficulty getting it... Why is that?

Many ancient scriptures tell us that everyone receives blessings. They claim that wealth and prosperity are our birth rights as humans. That if you live a good and humble life, if you obey this, or do that, you can expect fulfillment. However, these scriptures usually talk about these blessings in parables: cryptic messages hardly anyone understands. Some say that if you wish for something, it will be granted. Others say that you must affirm you want what you desire. This leads many of us to affirm "I want prosperity" or "I want ____________________ " (fill in the blank).

The tricky part is that when you claim you want something, your subconscious (the Infinite, God, Higher Self, the Universe - use the word that fits your belief system) takes your words at its literal meaning.

As a result, people get what they asked for: the deep desire of *wanting something that seems just out of reach.* When you receive precisely what you asked for, you may say: "Well, that *is* what I asked for, but that is *not* what I meant." And so you find yourself always wanting more. You also have many things going on inside your mind that you are unaware of. These other things are thoughts, words, and emotional responses from other people, hidden in your subconscious mind. Next I'm going to talk about the real reasons why we fail at manifesting wealth or our hearts desire.

The real reasons we fail at manifesting wealth

One of the most popular sayings in the world goes: "Money can't buy happiness." While this is definitely true, there is no denying the fact that while money might not be able to bring you eternal happiness, it can bring you a multitude of things some of which are essential to survival. There must be extremely few individuals in the world who don't care about the monetary aspect of things. If someone suddenly received a substantial amount of wealth, the chances of them rejecting it are extremely low.

Most of us strive to gain financial independence, with our goals in life being heavily dependent on how much money we have available. Furthermore as life progresses an individual's responsibilities also increase and again, the need to have a source of money is important. There are people who are trying to manifest wealth to meet these responsibilities while there are others who are trying to do so for personal satisfaction and comfort. Regardless of the reason for wanting and desiring wealth, manifesting wealth is a skill. A skill that everyone can learn.

You might be doing all the things which you have been told to do through books, videos or mentors but, it all seems to be a waste of time. The results just aren't appearing. The Law of Attraction basically states that an individual can attract abundance into their lives and this abundance isn't just limited to wealth but encompasses love, professional gain, friendship and the list goes on.

The Law of Attraction encourages people to believe that they can attract abundance into their lives as the Universe is abundant itself and so can be used as a source. Several techniques have been developed over time such as positive affirmations or strong beliefs and the practice of manifesting wealth has increased in recent years. Sometimes, people apply the techniques and strategies but can't seem to reach their financial goal. Why does this happen?

Believing you are undeserving

Money is a tricky thing. When you have it, you want it but if you have too much of it, you start feeling guilty. Something that seriously hinders the manifesting process is when an individual believes that they just don't deserve that much wealth. You may be trying to manifest wealth on the surface but in the subconscious level, you might be thinking that you shouldn't receive the amount of money you deserve. This is understandable to some extent as people might feel like they aren't putting in the required effort, compared to others who work much harder but have lesser money.

However, to truly manifest wealth, you need to move past this misconception and realize that everyone deserves the best. Also, another thing to keep in mind is that once you do receive the money that you desire, you might be able to use that for good thus benefiting others around you as well.

Being impatient

When you want something, especially money, you can't really help but be impatient. It's human nature. However, it can prove to be significantly detrimental towards your manifestation process.

We keep on telling ourselves that the money we want is just about to reach us when in fact, it might be some time away thus making the wait difficult and frustrating. Furthermore, if you are impatient, chances are that you keep on giving up on the process and pick up where you left off when you feel motivated again. There's no denying the strength it takes to keep the manifestation going at a steady pace but, when you keep in mind the end-result, things become much easier.

Try to remember that you have asked the Universe for some abundance so you yourself must be abundant with your patience in turn.

Vague idea of what you will do with the money

While coming into a significant amount of wealth will be welcomed by everyone, most of us aren't exactly sure what we will do with that money.

When manifesting wealth, you must have a clear idea of what the money will be used for. Will you buy a house? A car? Or do you just want to build your savings? Knowing what you are expecting to do from the wealth that you desire goes a long way in the resulting success of the process. Money needs to have a direction. Wealth needs to have a focus.

Another thing which tends to deter the process is when people think that they need more money to carry out a specific task when in fact, they already have the money they need. If this is the case, manifesting wealth which you might already have becomes near impossible. Before you attempt the manifestation process, try to look within and figure out how you can use the money you currently have and why you feel like you may need more.

Another thing to keep in mind when talking about the Law of Attraction and its role in manifesting wealth is that sometimes, you may feel that you want your life to go in a certain direction but the signs which the Universe are pointing towards are going in another direction.

Keep your eyes, minds and hearts open to all these signs and by re-evaluating your manifestation techniques with time, you will surely manage to achieve your goals. And lastly, looking at shutting out negative thoughts.

Shutting out the negative thoughts

One of the basic tips associated with manifesting wealth or any other abundance is remaining positive. Using affirmations and filling your mind with positive thoughts is often thought to be the key to a successful manifestation. However, you may still not be seeing the results.

This can happen when you are telling yourself what you are supposed to, but your mind is exactly listening. This happens when your negative thoughts are still swirling around in your head. How do you get rid of them though? Well, this isn't as straightforward as it sounds because negativity can enter our lives without any effort. And the opposite is true when it comes to positivity but, what you need to do is to address the negative thoughts.

Don't ignore them but dwell on them and ask yourself why these thoughts exist. Find ways to deal with the source of your negativity and your manifestation process becomes much easier. An easier way to understand how negative thoughts work in your life, let's look at what creates your current reality.

What Creates Your Current Reality?

There have been many studies, tests, and opinions as to *what* creates our current reality. The biggest breakthrough in this area was in the early 1900s by a pioneer in the field of "*Cognitive Behavior Modification.*" This ground-breaking work was developed by Dr. Thurman Fleet. His work in the realm of Concept-Therapy validated that, if a person changes their thinking, their entire life will change. I personally can validate this has been true in my life. This same theory has been expressed in numerous ways for thousands of years. It gets to the core of how your reality is created. To explain Dr. Fleet's findings, he used pictures of stick people to express how the active mind and how the subconscious mind works in creating our life experiences. In the following examples, I will show how our past has created our current results. This useful information is to give you an understanding of the mechanisms.

The subconscious mind creates our current reality from past input. It takes words at their literal meaning. Earlier I mentioned that when you *want* something that this creates a pattern of always *wanting*. This is because the word *want* implies an unfulfilled desire. The subconscious does not question ideas, and it does not understand what the word NO means. Your subconscious mind is unable to tell the difference between what is real and what is imagined.

The conscious mind is your thinking mind. It is the part of us that can be educated and allows your conscious choices to choose the thoughts, opinions, and ideas of others. The conscious mind programs the subconscious mind through the use of repetitive thoughts and input from experiences. The stronger your emotions are from an experience, the more deeply it is ingrained in your subconscious. This is why many of us are unaware of what is truly going on inside our minds. Especially if you have had traumatic experiences when you were younger. These experiences will continue to replay over and over, until we are able to resolve the first circumstance of the experiences. Once you heal from a fractured self, you are able to consciously choose different experiences.

There are many ways to integrate ourselves into wholeness. The methods I will walk you through will help you rewrite your subconscious mind with ease. There are many ways to rewrite the subconscious mind; there is not just one correct way. Some methods will work better than others for you. You can use relaxation techniques, such as meditation and hypnotherapy. You can use music; singing with the songs, making up your own, and/or using body movements and dancing. Or you can concentrate on affirmations, positive mantras, or play positive affirmations continuously in the background as you do other things. The stronger your desire to make the changes, the faster and more permanent these changes will be. After you have rewritten your desired programs, be aware of what you feed your mind with and do mental maintenance.

Many of us grew up with parents who did not know how to program their minds to create desirable results. My family was not taught how to change their reality. I was on my own by the time I was seventeen and had to figure it out. At the time, there was no internet, smartphones or massive book stores where I lived. I refused to live the reality that I grew up in, so I moved from my small town to the next largest city by the time I was eighteen. I am not suggesting you need to move for your changes. This is something I did, because I could not imagine living my life as the accepted normal of being *"barefoot and pregnant."* Even though I moved to a larger city, this belief was already ingrained in my mind. I became pregnant by the time I was twenty. I was able to buck this belief by working, but I still had a deeply ingrained poverty belief system that kept me on the edge of homelessness. When my son began to eat solid foods, my food supply decreased until I was buying crackers to feed him. I was angry and frustrated. Because I was working full time, we did not qualify for food stamps. According to the social system I grew up in, I was making too much money. However, I was not making enough to pay my rent and have food on the table. Credit cards were not generally accepted at grocery stores or for paying utilities. Regardless, I never allowed my son to go hungry. Many things went into my mind, until finally I felt this deep emotional pain that shattered my reality. It was then when I vowed that I would never be placed in this situation again. The very first step you need to take in order to change your circumstances is to make a decision that you will find solutions. This decision has to be strong enough for you to make it automatically when events come up to challenge you.

In this next section, I will lead you through valuable ways to help you get to the root of why your life may not be as you desire.

First let us take a look at where your thoughts are, and the feelings associated with those thoughts. Take a moment and think of your favorite childhood television show. Mine was *Gilligan's Island*. I can still hear the theme song playing. I remember I used to feel sad every time those castaways nearly made it off the island, only to have something go wrong and fail again. Do you remember the show *Cheers*? Maybe your favorite show was *Knight Rider*? Perhaps you remember *Gun Smoke* or *Howdy Doody*. As I mentioned earlier, the higher the emotional response is to an experience, the deeper it goes into the subconscious. This is one reason some people cannot shake their childhood traumas or nightmares from watching horror movies. Some things our parents or other people we cared about said to us as children, we interpreted as disapproval; now we attempt to get approval from everyone. We may respond with fear of conflict, or by pleasing others while placing our own well-being on the back shelf.

What feelings do you have when you think of your favorite shows? You thought about a show and now you have feelings from that thought. Interesting, isn't it? Perhaps sometimes you remember snapshots and scenes, but cannot remember which movie or show they come from. Think of your favorite restaurant commercial. Can you almost *taste* your favorite dish? Does your mouth water? Do you feel hungry?

Did you notice that first you thought about your favorite dish, next you felt your mouth water, and then you felt a bit hungry? This process is almost instantaneous and, if you do not pay attention, you might think you were hungry first. If you experienced any of the memories or feelings I mentioned, I would like to congratulate you! You are an A+ plus student! You have learned that your mind can be fed something and retain it for many years… even a lifetime.

Now, think of your mind as a lush garden, or an amazing computer that receives input, retains this input, and gives you an output. You may be more selective about what you put into your garden or computer (meaning your mind) these days. When you were younger, you really had no idea which input was good and which one was bad. You were curious about the world around you and wanted to learn everything. You learned from your environment, caregivers, friends, school, and so forth. All the bad input you took in during that time affected your programming, but you do have the power to unlearn what you learned. I commend you for taking the first step creating the fabulous business and lifestyle you have always desired. It is not as hard as you might think: you only have to rewrite your programs once, and then be careful what you choose to take in to perform the maintenance. It is really not that difficult after you get going. Your mind is a muscle. At first, when you start to actively do different exercises that you are not used to, you may experience some resistance. This fades into a feeling of being refreshed and excited about what you will be choosing to create next!

Let us begin with a simple exercise to look at what you have learned from past experiences, so you can identify these as your current personal thoughts and feelings. These are usually behaviors, thoughts, words, and actions from others, though they may be hard to recognize. Imagine you are about to do something that one of your childhood care providers would disapprove of. Do you still feel a bit uneasy? Did you hear *their words* in your head?

Let us see what is really going on in your mind.

Exercise 1: The Garden Exercise

Grab your journal or use the space below and write down the answers to the following. Envision your mind as a garden. Close your eyes and take a couple of deep breaths. Ask yourself: "What is in my mental garden?"

Open your eyes and write everything you sense, see, feel or hear.

____

____

____

____

____

____

____

____

____

This garden exercise helps you find out what is on the surface of your subconscious; did you find surprising things came up?

The next exercise will help you discover what is even deeper in your subconscious than what you just discovered on the surface.

Exercise 2: The Index Card Exercise

You need a 3" x 5" index card, a notepad application on your cell phone, or a journal. Make sure that you will have access to whatever you decide to use for the next six days.

Write a date at the top of the card. Under the date make four columns. Label the first column Positive, the next Negative, the third Happy, and the last Sad. Feel free to use other words.

This is how I made mine:

Positive	Negative	Happy	Sad	Date

This method is for you to track your thoughts and how they make you feel. Note it on the card. I like to use tallies (like this: ⅢⅠ) to keep track of mine, but you can use whatever suits your style. If you have a strong response to the thought, write it on the back of the card. This helps you to know where you are starting from, so that you know where you want to go. It would be difficult to get to your destination if you did not know your starting point.

For the first three days, observe your thoughts and mark your card or track them using the method of your choice. For the following three days, every time you think of something you do not like or would not want to manifest, gently push on the spot between your eyebrows with your index finger. This spot is between the eyebrows at the top of the bridge of your nose. It is below your third eye chakra. Gently use this eject spot for any unwanted thoughts for which the other methods did not work. Push it as many times as you want. However, be gentle when you do. Consciously say a word such as "stop," "eject," or "cancel." You can also say: "Get out of my head!"; whatever you feel would be most effective. Then make a mark on your card.

If your mind has racing thoughts you cannot control, place your right hand on your right ear and your left hand on your left ear. Say in a strong commanding voice: "Be Silent!" You may have to do this several times in a row, several times a day, until your mind quiets down enough to eject the unwanted thoughts.

Remember: your mind, like a muscle, will respond to commands. Once you get a handle on negative or racing thoughts, your life will start to flow with more ease and grace. This is because you will become more aware of what is going on around you, and you can take action beforehand. I know this to be true. As an example: because my mind became quieter, I was able to notice that my car was making an unusual sound. This saved me from potentially being stranded, because I took my car to a shop. They found an issue with the spark plug misfiring, which meant my car might not start properly at any given moment. As your mind becomes quieter, you become more aware. This can literally save your life. As you become more proactive about your thoughts and feelings, you will notice slight changes in your environment. The slight changes will continue and, eventually, you will notice some major changes. Sometimes, but not always, these changes may look or feel a little chaotic. This is natural. The rational left side of your conscious mind does not like change that much. Hang tight as it is a sure sign that good things are coming your way, but negative things need to be cleared away.

At times, we tend to lose focus because we are too busy worrying about the negativity in our lives. Here is something that would help:

What did you accomplish today? Write it down below (it doesn't matter how simple it was):

As you become more positive, your energy vibrates at a higher frequency. Higher frequency emotions are known as love, gratitude, kindness, peace, wealth, prosperity, and so forth. The lower vibrations are associated with anger, depression, fear, hatred, and so forth. Your thoughts directly affect how you feel. As you raise your positive thoughts, you will no longer resonate with situations that are of a lower vibration. You may notice that the Universe is clearing negativity out of your life. This may include people, places, and things that no longer serve you. Understand that good things are on their way to you, even if things do not appear that way. Everything has a divine order to it, and this helps you to return to a space where your balance is restored. Your natural state is to be happy, healthy, and wealthy. Watch children playing, laughing, and enjoying themselves; you will remember that you were once like that too. When you take control of your thoughts and rewrite what is in your subconscious, you return to your natural state of being.

If you notice that your negative thoughts catch you off guard or you are starting to feel irritable and cranky, you are bumping up against a strong belief system. Continue to work with these thoughts, but this time take a moment and ask this feeling when was the first time you felt this way. This may take you to a different time when you were younger or maybe to a different landscape altogether. Stay with it, and allow yourself to validate this feeling. This is when your thoughts catch you off guard. You may start to berate yourself. You may tell yourself that you are stupid and that you 'should have' known better. Move deeper into this 'should have' feeling and ask it again when was the first time you felt it. This time, allow yourself to go there with compassion for yourself. Allow yourself to state: "I made a mistake, and I forgive myself for making an error. Everyone makes mistakes. I pardon my error from this point forward."

Now, imagine yourself moving to the present moment, allowing yourself to be free from your own judgments. Notice that this feels constricting and you are able to be more caring toward yourself and others around you. As you become more conscious of your thoughts, you will notice how quickly they form your reality around you. When you change your thoughts, your world begins to mold itself to the new signals you are sending out into it.

Notes:

Notes:

Chapter 8

CHANGE YOUR THOUGHTS AND CHANGE YOUR WORLD

Imagine your mind as a garden again. Imagine your negative thoughts are *weeds* that have run amuck in your lush beautiful garden. Imagine going through it and pulling the weeds that have taken over your garden. These weeds represent negative thoughts that you have had. Imagine you are tossing these weeds into a burning barrel or an incinerator, so they will not return or be able to reproduce. Now, envision the areas where you pulled out the weeds as fresh fertile soil where you can now choose what you desire to plant. You can choose a vegetable garden, fruit trees, beautiful flowers, and anything else that entices you. This new garden will be able to sprout and bloom into a lush oasis that brings you untold prosperity, wealth, abundance, or whatever you desire. Yes, you can have it all. You may not be able to have it all at once, but you will be able to have your truest heart's desires. If you think that having it all is not possible, or that it would require having to make a trade off, that thought is a tricky little weed. You can have anything you truly desire if you are steadfast without wavering. You can think of this as eating a meal. You would not want to eat an entire months' worth of food in one sitting, nor would you be able to handle everything you desired all at once. Some thoughts are a bit tricky to determine if they are really weeds. If you notice a thought is an "if I have this, then that will happen," it is a tricky thought of an "either or" mindset (a weed). This learned behavior will demolish your self-esteem in subtle ways. And it can demoralize you into doing sabotaging behaviors that go unnoticed by you. As an example of the "If this, then that," thoughts usually show up as: if you do the "right thing" or "play your cards right," then you will be rewarded with what you want. The trick is that you are believing in a distortion of the truth. You get what you want some of the time, reinforcing this distortion, but it tricks you out of things that would lead to major breakthroughs for you.

At times, it is difficult to change your thoughts because of some unpleasant memories. Here is something to help you in that regard:

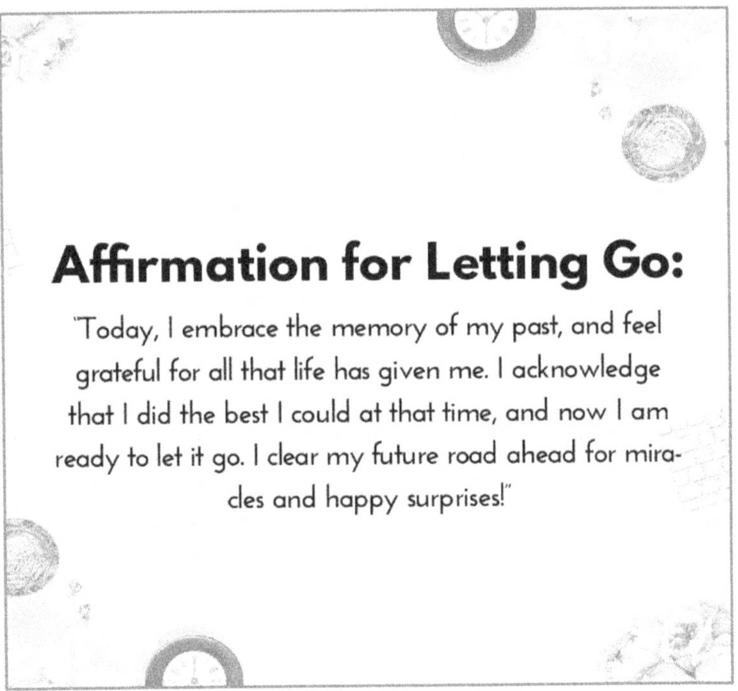

Other dangerous thoughts are either A or B. These thoughts are similar to the above, but it separates your total good from coming to you. It is like telling a child that they can only have vanilla ice cream or chocolate ice cream, but they cannot mix them together to make a twist. This becomes distorted, as you become an adult, into an "either this or that" mentality. An example that many of my clients have expressed is: "I have to choose between working long hours to make good money or spending time with my family." Can you see how these kinds of thoughts lead you down an exhausting path of guilt, shame, and frustration? Thousands of people are living full lives while working reasonable hours. They have a joyful career or business while experiencing wealth, happiness, and success, *and* they have plenty of time with their families.

Returning to your beautiful garden. Imagine placing seeds for lush vibrant plants and name them for things you desire.

For example, plant a row of trees and name them 'your money trees'. You can plant golden potatoes and name them 'for receiving treasures of gold'. You can have fun while using an affirmation to represent each seed you plant.

Some affirmations I use include:

I am happy, healthy, wealthy and wise.

Whenever I give money, it recirculates back to me.

I receive money from everywhere and everyone.

My 'goodness' now sprouts and bloom in my life.

Everyday in Every Way I am Blessed.

I am open to receive that which is mine by divine right and divine selection.

More prosperity flows into my life than goes out.

I allow myself the treasures of my soul to flow to me today.

Wherever I be, whatever I do, prosperity flows easily to me.

I see abundance all around me and I open my arms to receive it.

Money flows abundantly to me. I open my hands and see it right before me now.

I am consistently presented with new opportunities and success.

Today is rich with opportunities and I open my heart to receive them.

I am one with my source and abundance comes to me effortlessly.

It is my time now and I am ready for the next step.

Every day and every way I am getting better and better.

Today, I claim that which is mine by divine right and I open wide to receive.

I step into my new chosen life with ease and with grace.

I have all the time, money, and energy to do whatever I choose.

If you need more ideas for positive affirmations, search YouTube and the internet. You will find affirmations for nearly any area you can think of. I personally find all kinds of affirmations, hypnosis audios, and much more from using keywords in the YouTube or Google search bar. You can also purchase any of the numerous books on affirmations. The key is to put emotion behind the affirmations. Saying affirmations in a dry non-emotional tone will not take hold or, if they do, they will be very weak. Remember: experiences with a high emotional charge and response go deeper into the subconscious where your reality is created from. To get yourself in a happier state before you start using your affirmations, listen to uplifting music, dance, sing, or watch videos. Do whatever it takes to make yourself feel happier. You have the power to change your world and start experiencing freedoms, money, and joy beyond your wildest dreams. Start today, and everyday reaffirm that you will continue. When this becomes a daily habit, you will notice changes happening fast.

Now that you have an idea of what is currently in your mind and your garden, you can make changes much easier. You have affirmations to help you, and you have the options of what you would like to manifest first. To start testing your manifesting ability, begin with simple things that would be easy to obtain. As you build your manifestation muscle, you can move into more elaborate desires. The reason you start with smaller desires is so you are able to start having more faith. Get or make a vision board. Place what you desire on one side and note what you have manifested on the other side. Use post-it notes that you can move from the desire side of the board to the manifested side of the board. This visual aid will help you feel more in control of creating the life you desire, rather than living by default and reacting to everything that shows up. You have the power to choose to respond with grace and ease, or react with emotional turmoil.

What seeds of desire do you want to plant for the future?

Exercise 3: The Paradigm Exercise

Grab your journal and write down the answers to the following:

List what you would like to plant in your garden: who you want to become and what you want to be, what you want to do, and what you want to have. This is your *BE, DO and HAVE* list. It is important that you start this list with what and who do you want to be. From a state of being, state what you desire to do. Finally, from being and doing, what you desire to have. The masculine paradigm is the "have, do, be." This is starting to fade as competition is fading into cooperation. We are moving into a time of the feminine energy where we start to nurture ourselves. From the space of being, we then do, and as a result, we have. This new paradigm is more natural to the way the world really works, and will result in your inner cup flowing over. This flow will allow you to give from the spaciousness of abundance, rather than from a space of depletion.

Go back to the index card exercise and take some time to look over your index cards. Ask yourself: "Is this really what I want in my life?" "Are my current thoughts and feelings what I desire?" With this exercise, you will be able to observe and discover the root of issues, so you can change them. Do not feel bad if your random thoughts do not yet reflect your true desires for your business or lifestyle. For many years, you accepted other people's belief systems, paradigms, and bad behaviors toward yourself. You have been in a fog of sorts for a long time; you were not aware of these things going on in your mind. Go easy on yourself, because you are in a learning curve. Plus, you have to acknowledge that you are truly an A+ plus student.

Continue to use the index cards; cancel every thought you do not desire and replace it with one you do. Use the positive affirmations mentioned previously or come up with your own. You can use generic ones such as: "Good things are happening to me all the time" or "Even though I may fear change, I allow myself to explore the good things in life." Use positive affirmations first thing when you wake up and right before you go to bed for maximum effect. Put positive affirmations on YouTube or your cell phone and play them in the background as you get ready for your day. Avoid watching negative stories or the news in the morning and before bed. This is the time where you are most likely to be programmed.

You may feel more tired than usual. This is normal, as you are *rewriting* the programs that have been running in your subconscious mind for a long time. It may be a bit hard at the beginning, but do not give up. I promise you that it does get easier as you continue.

Eventually, you will only have to do maintenance. Keep up the good work and forgive yourself quickly if you fall off the positive mindset bandwagon.

Persistence always wins. This is a lifestyle change. It is not something that you do a few times and you are done. Watch as your life starts to change bit by bit. Focus on the little changes that excite you. Look for and appreciate the ways in which the Universe is bringing good into your life. You are a creator, and this book will help you as an instruction manual. Use these signs for motivation to keep going at it. Especially keep going when things are at their all-time best. When we start to slip back into our old habits or mindsets, we start to unknowingly lose things. I have made this error several times, and it is painful when your slipping leads to an avalanche before you know it.

You have a new lease on life, and you can go in any direction you would like. This process will open you to your infinite possibilities.

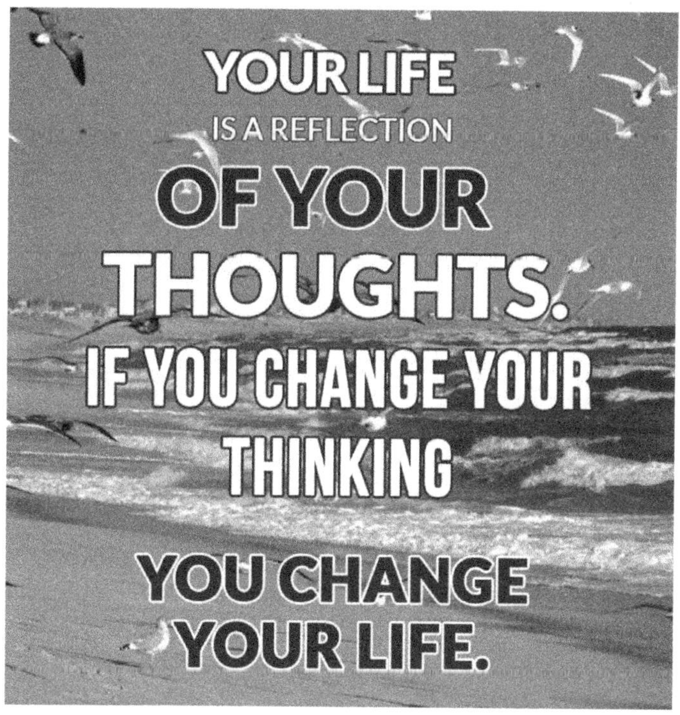

Remember: you become what you think and believe. Your thoughts (both known and *unknown*) create the experiences in your life. Listen carefully to what you *say* consciously and *un*consciously. This will help shape your entire world. You will start to believe your positive affirmations and life affirming statements. Be consistent, and work at it daily, to reap the greatest results. Beliefs are thoughts you think over and over that have an emotional charge to them. You can disarm these charges by changing your beliefs through consistent work.

Your point of power is in this very moment. When you become distracted with thoughts of the past or worries about tomorrow, you are not in your point of power. Stop yourself and listen to your breath. Remind yourself: "All is well in my world in this moment." Now is the time to realize how powerful your thoughts really are and how they create both your feelings and your perceptions of the world around you. This process shifts you from reacting with emotion to responding with ease. From each point of power, you can create your fate by default through random thoughts, or you can consciously design your desired business and lifestyle with ease. Conscious creation will empower you to notice an abundance of opportunities, and this noticing will provide clues to your destiny. You are here with a divine mission, and you *do* have a purpose. As your life unfolds, you can choose to live it by design, rather than by default.

If you become overwhelmed, take a few moments to breathe and give yourself permission to stop for a few hours. Then decide to work harder until you see more results in your life. The results could include more money, sales or creative ideas, better self-care or relationships, or whatever success feels like to you. Sometimes, feeling overwhelmed is a natural response to change and to an overabundance of choices. You have become accustomed to your automatic ways of thinking and reacting. This work will help you discover other ways, which you can choose to adopt or adapt to your desires. With all change, even good change, there is a certain amount of distress and confusion. Remember: it has taken much of your life to *learn* how to feel small and powerless, take things personally, lose self-respect, and allow others to dishonor you. Some of these may not apply to you; perhaps you have learned how to be an overachiever or a perfectionist. If you are reading this, I am certain that you will be able to create lasting changes in your life. This is not some crazy method that I just thought up by myself. I have, however, thoroughly time-tested it for over twenty years. You can find books on this that go back several hundred years. It is not taught by the mainstream. Even if you have watched movies on the Law of Attraction, they omit to tell you about the other circumstances required for that one law to work for your greater good.

You may have spent years living the good child complex, where you think you should be happy with what you have because "things could be worse." But you still feel a void or emptiness inside that you just cannot shake. It is that part of you that wants to be bigger, brighter, and happier than ever. You are looking for answers, because your true self, your soul self, is waking up. You are questioning the way things have been arranged in your business and life. You are resisting the system and the years of programming imposed on you by others. This programming has kept you in a state of suspended animation, but you feel like you are coming back to life. This is because you are waking up to infinite possibilities and your personal truth. Until now, you forgot how to be a divine spiritual being that is abundant and rich with infinite possibilities and has all the resources needed to succeed available. To keep bringing your soul self back to life, continue working on these exercises. When you feel that you no longer need the index cards, continue to use a journal and document your journey. Keep track of your grandest dreams; remember to write down your accomplishments and celebrate each new step you take. You never know when these journals will become a best-selling book. Most of the work in this book is from articles I have written, trainings I created, and from my own personal journals. This work has empowered many individuals to attain more money and freedom, while experiencing more joy than ever before. Once you discover where you are starting from, you are able to start moving toward having wealth consciousness.

In the next section, I will be discussing how we develop our beliefs about money, wealth, and prosperity and what you can do to develop these.

Notes:

Chapter 9

AN INTRODUCTION TO WEALTH CONSCIOUSNESS

Throughout most of history, there has been a perceived contrast between those who have wealth and those who do not. This separation became more and more of a gap as the world became industrialized. Another gap is the division between men and women when it comes to earning money. Traditions are fading away, as more and more women are taking ownership of their money and wealth. Currently, there are more women becoming entrepreneurs than in the past. These women are bringing cooperation and collaboration to the world, instead of the formerly accepted competition. You may be one of them.

The struggles many of us face when it comes to money, stem from false belief systems, half-truths, and misunderstandings. Money is necessary, and so is wealth. It is easier to use coins and paper money as payment for goods and services, than it is to exchange grains, gold, or produce. Money has been called many things and, mostly, it symbolizes power. This perceived power has been used to harm others in numerous ways. As the world begins to change, this former system is in the process of being dismantled. Many may see this as doom and gloom, but it is a necessary step to bring forth new beliefs and shape the world in a new fashion. Money is simply the acceptable means of exchange, but many of us fear having too much money because we fear that people will hate us. You may feel like this. Money is a neutral device by itself. It is the value that people have placed on it that makes it valuable. Many have placed a lot of connotations on money and what it really means. We use money in society today as a form of energy exchange for the use of goods and services. This system was devised so we could exchange goods and services around the world. Imagine not being able to go to another state or country, because there was no form of exchange for value. You would be stuck in the area in which you were born and would have a very difficult time trying to move from one area to the next. As you start thinking about money and what money means to you personally, you will discover what your wealth consciousness is. You develop a wealth consciousness similarly to how you develop your other belief systems. You may place a higher value on money than it deserves, or you may place a lower value on it.

In this introduction to wealth consciousness, I will take you through several exercises, so you can start having a healthier relationship with money. These methods have worked for me and thousands of women I have taught. It is my deepest desire that they will get you started toward creating more money, freedom, and joy in your life with ease. This book alone is not meant to be the one and only book you ever read regarding creating more money in your life. It is complementary to other studies, and can be used alongside your own ideas about money. It is not, by any means, an all-in-one. There are so many good books written about money, that you could create a library. My money story was created by the experiences I have had since I was a toddler.

Notes:

Chapter 10

MY MONEY STORY

Shortly before I was three years old, my half-sister, Vicky, drowned while filling up squirt guns on the frozen river. Father was already an alcoholic with a mean streak. After this tragedy, he was unable to bear the pain he felt, and became enraged. His suffering was so great, that he lashed out at my mother; eventually, he started to lash out at my sister and me. My mother was left with no choice; she filed for a divorce. This left her with little money to raise two little girls. She had no skills, education or means. She worked day and night trying to make ends meet. This started to form my money story: you have to work really hard and long hours to make enough to survive. My family was on government assistance most of my life. I am grateful we were never homeless nor without some form of food. My mom believed that you could not earn a good living without graduating from high school or having a college education. Even after she obtained a certificate from our local community college. The absolutely most my mom ever made in one year was $24,000 and it was only once. She usually made far less. We were so poor that she had to hand make my clothes, as fabric was cheaper than purchasing clothes from the store. I remember how embarrassed I felt not having blue jeans when everyone else wore them. I began working odd jobs by the time I was nine. The only conversations we ever had about money were that we did not have enough or we could not afford something I wanted.

Studies have shown that women worry that talking about money will make them vulnerable, make someone feel bad, or feel like they are crossing a social boundary. You may be feeling vulnerable right now. This vulnerability is part of your money story. Despite the fact that 92 percent of the women studied wanted to learn more about money, 80 percent refrained from discussing money, even with their family. This was the case with our family. This feeds into the fear women have regarding their own financial future. You may be a woman who fears talking about money and your financial future. This money story will keep you from reaching the heights of true freedom and true joy in your life. It may prevent you from having the success you so deeply desire.

My childhood experiences created these money stories for me:

Money is hard to get.

You have to do things you do not want to do to get money.

You have to be at the mercy of another person to get money.

Girls have to work twice as hard to make money.

If you have money, the government will take it from you.

You have to work hard and give up your health for wealth.

You cannot enjoy time with your family, because you have to work to pay the bills.

You have to give up things you desire, just to survive.

You had better make a lot of money if you want "that."

Do not dream too big, as you will be disappointed.

Better get it now because prices will go up.

Rich people had to swindle somebody to make their money.

Only large corporations have money, and it is a dog eat dog world.

If you do not have a higher education, you will not make any money.

You have to shrink your dreams down to the size of your paycheck.

College is for rich people.

Your Money Story

You may have similar money stories as mine. These money stories directly affect your wealth consciousness. You may have ones that are more restrictive. Let us find out what your money stories are, so you can transform them from ones that prevent you from succeeding to ones that empower you.

You will need peace and quiet for this exercise. It is best to be in an area where you will not be disturbed; put your phone on silent and put it in another room.

Exercise: The Money Story Exercise

Grab you journal and some different colored pens. Answer the following questions. Do not take a lot of time answering them. Write down the first thing that pops into your mind after you read the question. Write this down, even if it does not make sense to you:

When you were growing up, what lessons did you learn about money from your Mother?

What types of experiences did she have and what choices did she make?

What was her perception about money and how did she manage or not manage it?

Take a few deep breaths before answering the next set of questions.

When you were growing up, what lessons did you learn about money from your Father?

What experiences did he have and choices did he make?

What was his perception of money and how did he managed or not managed it?

____

____

____

____

____

Did your parents or caregivers talk or argue about money around you? If so, what do you believe you heard and how did you understand it?

What were the comments, beliefs, and messages you received from your other relatives? Such as your Aunts, Uncles, Grandparents, etc.

Look at what you just wrote down about money and how it was talked about, handled, or otherwise. How do you feel this has affected your own money story? Were there other experiences you had as a child that involved money? Note this responses in your journal.

____

____

____

Based on your Money Story exercise, what do you believe is your current money story? Do you have a better or worse money story than your parents? Now that you have an idea of what your money story is, are you willing to change your money story to one that is more empowering for you? Even if you have a good money story, would you like to have a better one?

Whatever your answers, you can start this process by writing: *"Yes! I want to have more money, wealth, and prosperity in my life!"* in your journal.

Understanding Your Money Relationship

When you understand your perceptions about your money story, you can understand the type of relationship you have with money. Understanding is the starting point for improving your life and finances. Many of the questions in this book are meant to trigger a response in your mind, so it begins allowing you to alter a negative belief about money into a positive feeling about money. When we have a positive feeling or expectancy about money, we are able to create more in our lives. As you continue through the rest of this book, keep your journal nearby so you can jot down notes and responses.

Take a moment, close your eyes, and breathe in deeply. Start to feel where in your body you have a money issue or story. Feel if there are any tingling sensations, aches or pains. After you locate them, start to breathe deeper into each area of your body that has been affected. Do you feel like you have been wounded by money or the misuse of money? Continue to breathe deeper into this area and be willing to forgive money itself for this wound. In reality, it was not money by itself that created this harm; it was another person or company that made you feel this way. Allow yourself to have intense feelings, if you need to, but keep going back to forgiving the energy and the currency of money. You do not have to forgive the person at this moment. You may have some intense feelings come up. Stay with them and go deeper. Imagine these intense feelings are little bubbles coming to the surface from underwater and popping as they hit the air.

Open your journal and write down your experiences. Ask yourself these questions and write down the answers:

Did these experiences create a sense of anxiety around money?

Have these experiences affected how you manage money?

Do they negatively impact other relationships?

Before making a quick decision, ask your body if you are open to receive more money, wealth, and abundance into your life. Feel into the answer. Our minds will always say a quick "yes," but going deeper you will discover the truth that is stored in your body.

In order to be open to receiving money into your life, you need to be open to receive. To find out how well you receive, close your eyes and imagine one of your best friends giving you a very expensive gift that you were not expecting. How does that make you feel? Are you happy? Do you wonder how your friend could possibly afford this gift? Do you feel like you do not deserve it?

Now imagine you are that friend, and you have purchased an incredible gift for one of your friends. Imagine wrapping this gift in the most beautiful paper you can find; it looks perfect in every aspect. How do you feel when you give this gift to your friend? Do you feel different when you give it than when you receive it? If you feel it is better to give than receive, this directly affects your money story.

If you had some negative thoughts or feelings from this receiving exercise, or if you have a previous money story, you may have created a money monster or "boogieman" in your mind and in your life. Living with these creatures lurking in our subconscious mind is like walking in a land mine field. You never know what will trigger a response that leads you to making emotionally based decisions that crush your financial potential. You also lose freedoms, and it sucks all the joy in your life. You may be living with outdated rules of society rules. This triggers you to be reserved and hold back; it prevents you from truly expressing yourself. There is hope, and you can change this starting today.

Notes:

Chapter 11

WHAT IS A MONEY "BOOGIEMAN?"

The money boogie man can be related to any area of your life. You can use the exercises and tips to relate it to the area you decide you need help with.

When you think of money and your current relationship with money, do you feel like money is a monster that you love to hate? I completely understand. I grew up with a fear of money, because it was what "those" people used against poor people like me. I always felt there was some kind of division between me and them. This "us against them" mentality is very destructive. Beliefs like these taint and distort our views regarding what money really is. You may be mistaking people's actions around money for what money is. This leads you into making money the bad guy, the monster, or what I call "your money boogieman." You may have good feelings and relationships regarding money. You may feel you do not have any money boogiemen in your mental shelf. But stay with me and complete the following exercise. It covers another area you would like to have closure for once and for all.

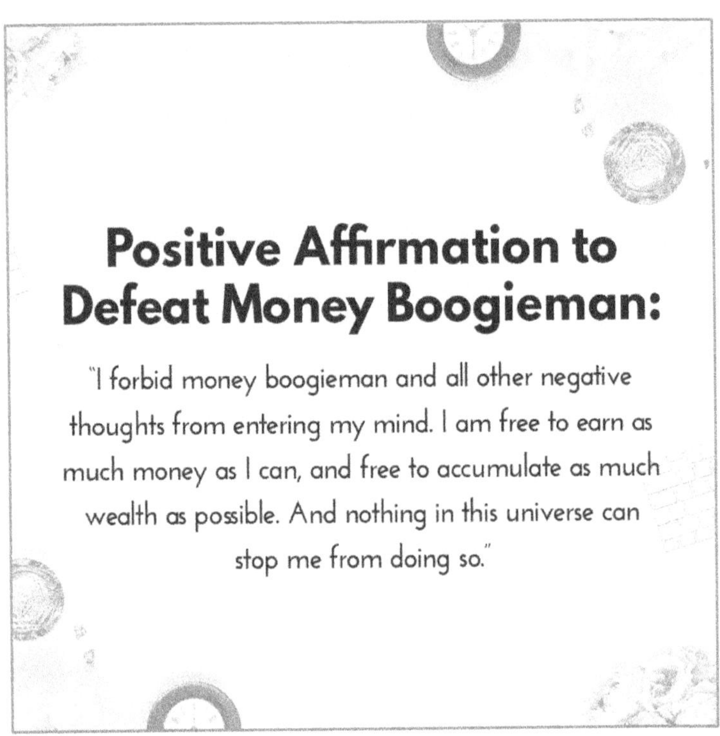

Destroying the Money Boogieman

In order to truly get rid of the money boogieman and the money stories that you created since you were a child, you need to take time for yourself to be alone. You can do this with your partner, if you desire, but I recommend you do this alone first. You can plan to do this a second time with your partner about a month after each of you have completed your first round.

You can adapt this following ritual to get rid of anything you want, so be creative if you need to do this more than once, that's fine. Sometimes, you may need to do this on several different subjects and topics. Other times, you may need to revisit doing this again to destroy a new Boogieman that arises.

Be sure you are in a safe place where you will not be disturbed. Decide and plan this for when you will be able to be alone. If you have any pets, be sure they are put away in a safe place where they cannot jump on you or scratch on the door. If you have children, arrange for them to be at a different location for at least an hour or two. Leave the laundry and dishes if you must. This would not be a good time to multitask. Turn off your cell phone. If you are going to be outside, do your best to be alone and in an area where you can have a small fire for a few minutes. Nothing ruins this letting-go faster than someone intruding in your space and asking questions. Or teasing you about toasting marshmallows. As you prepare for this, be sure you carry through with this from start to finish. If you get the supplies, but then wait for the perfect time, it will never happen. You have to schedule this to make it happen.

It may sound silly. I admit that the first time I did mine, I was more than skeptical. I was also experiencing so much suffering, that I was willing to suspend my former training and know-it-all attitude. I clearly did not know-it-all or I would have not been in the circumstances I was in. I hope you are not in the pain and suffering I was in, but, if you are, this will work better. It is the beginning of reclaiming your life and finances, regardless of how silly it may appear at first.

Supplies you will need:

One wide tip black marker

A box of crayons or multiple colored pens and pencils. Any number of colors will work, even if you only have a few.

Blank white paper. Copy or printer paper works well.

A fireplace or fireproof container that is in a safe area.

A long nose lighter. The barbeque lighters work well.

This is your time now, and it is important that you go through this process to its completion, or you may feel that you are not finished. Or worse yet, your money boogie man will come back with a vengeance and catch you off guard.

Now, take in a few deep breaths and close your eyes. Prepare to be truly honest with yourself as best as you are able to at this time. After you open your eyes, think of all the ways you have felt abandoned by money. Think of all the times other people have used money against you. Think about all the toys you never got for Christmas. Think about how so many people in your life have had arguments about money, or were so angry that they were silent and ignored you when you asked questions. Feel the emotions you had when you were told No over and over again; when you were at the store or any other place you were not allowed to have what you wanted. Now grab the paper and a colored crayon or pen and start writing down how this made you feel. You do not have to write correct sentences. You can make words, symbols, sad faces, or you scribble on the page. Think of how angry you are at not having the money you want to live your life the way you want to live it. Scribble, write, draw some more. Get more into this project and grab different colors as you desire. If you have to get up and stomp around, jump up and down or yell, do so. Do return to the paper when you are done and grab another color and continue. Imagine putting all your hurt feelings, your tears, your fears, and your rage into the colors on this paper.

This will not be a pretty looking picture. This picture represents all the times you had to say No because you lacked money. All the times you cried yourself to sleep at night worrying about paying your bills. It is about expressing the shame you felt when you could not afford to get your family gifts or the kind of gifts you wanted. Place all the times you felt embarrassed, ashamed, belittled, and anxious about money into this paper.

Be bold, dramatic, and erratic with each stroke of color on the paper. Let all the chaos out of your mind and body, and put it into this paper. If you need to use the back side, do so. If you need to use several sheets, do so. Do whatever you have to do to place all the hardships you have faced into the paper. Think of how others treated you when you felt you did not have the money. Think of the times you have had ragged underclothes or patches on your clothes.

Consider putting into this paper all the times you heard yourself or your parents say:

"I would love to, but I cannot afford it."
"We do not have the money for that."

or

"You are crazy for wanting that!"

Think of the times you were told you cannot "make money doing that."

Keep scribbling until you can no longer think of any of the times you stayed in jobs you hated or worked for low wages with abusive bosses. Think of all the things that you have done just to squeak by, while watching others living the life that you desired.

Feel free to talk to this paper as if you are talking to the spirit of money. Give yourself a voice about money, and tell it all the things you ever wanted to tell it.

You can say things like:

"I felt really hurt when you abandoned me!"
"I am angry because you betrayed me!"
"You are a scoundrel. I hate the way you made me feel and I am going to get rid of you today!"

As you color on the page, bring forth all your anger and rage. Let it all flow out and make a mess on the paper. As you finally let out the last bit of your rage, you will start to feel a calming effect inside. You may feel a bit tired, or you may feel fully energized.

When you are completely satisfied with the page and you feel all your anger, frustration, loneliness, hurt, and pain has left you, pick up the large black marker and place an X from corner to corner on this page.

As you write this X on the paper – state firmly, boldly, and with authority:

"I cancel all debt! I delete all poverty!"
"I demolish all hurt feelings and I destroy this boogie man once and for all!"
"You no longer have possession of my mind or my affairs!"

Feel free to state whatever else you feel like stating.

Now, rip up this paper with vigor into tiny pieces and put them in the fireplace with the flue open or in your fireproof bucket. If you are inside and using a bucket, go outside before you set them on fire.

Set the papers on fire and say:

"I now renounce all scarcity from me and mine, today."
"I burn away all poverty and leave no residue."
"To lack-of-money, I bid you farewell."
"Gone forever is my strife and now I cancel all strife."
"Struggle no more shall I endure!"
"I renounce poverty and scarcity once more."
"Be gone from my life now and forevermore!"

Add any other sentence you desire.

The most important statement from above is to renounce scarcity and poverty from your life. After the ashes have cooled and it is safe to touch them, you can scatter them to the winds, bury them, put them in a river, or flush them. If none of these are an option and you used a fireplace, place the ashes in trash bag and dispose of them outside.

You are doing this in a physical manner, because your subconscious mind uses symbols and symbolism for communication. Words are normally translated by the conscious mind. Taking physical actions reinforces your decision to stop suffering financially from this point forth. It shows your inner self that you really mean business.

What to do if the Money Boogieman tries to return

As with all bad romances, sometimes the Money Boogieman tries to weasel its way back into your life. You will know this by small signs here and there. You will start to get anxious about money again. You might get concerned about purchasing basic items, such as food or paying for your living expenses. Sometimes it is subtler, and you catch yourself feeling uncomfortable accepting gifts. You may start to think: "I would love to have that, but I cannot afford it." (in which case, say to yourself: "That would be nice, but I have allocated my finances elsewhere at this time.")

So, what do you do if the money boogieman tries to return? You certainly do not want poverty consciousness back into your life... This exercise works like a charm every time; all of the time. Start by sitting quietly for a few moments and envision your Money Boogieman as a foul looking creature. Stare directly into its beady little eyes and bring it up close to you so that you are almost nose to nose. Feel yourself taking complete control of the situation. If you need to imagine yourself growing to ten feet tall so you are bending down to stare at this creature eye to eye, do so. Take in a long deep breath and, with all of your might, imagine expelling fire-like breath on this creature until it starts to shrink.

With each breath you exhale, see it shrinking smaller and smaller, until it is about an inch or two tall. Laugh and giggle as you bend down and pick this tiny creature up and place it in the palm of your other hand. Hold your hand up to the height of your mouth and give it a good sharp blow. Imagine it being sent out into orbit beyond the skies and into outer space. If you want to get creative, you can imagine it going into a black hole. Affirm strongly and boldly: "I now command you to go into orbit in peace, never to return here again! I renounce all poverty and lack from my life now and forevermore!"

Notes:

Chapter 12

MONEY MAGIC SPELLS

There is no right or wrong way to create a magical money spell. Some spells work better for some than others. Find one that resonates with you and use it as long as it feels fun, fresh and new to you. The following money spells are from various places, teachers, from my personal experience and from online too.

You can change around the words, delete, add or modify any spell.

These money spells are designed to help you tap into this natural flow and manifest abundance, so your life is filled with ease, contentment, luxury, and ever-increasing riches.

Clearing blocks to prosperity

This money spell will help you clear blocks to wealth, such as negative beliefs, limiting family paradigms, paralyzing fears, past-life patterns, and internalized cultural messages.

Ingredients

- A white candle and candle holder
- 1/4 cup sea salt
- An orange, cut into eight pieces

On the full moon or when the moon is waning, draw a bath. Light the candle and turn out any electric lights. Add the salt and the orange to the bathwater and stir with your dominant hand in a counterclockwise direction for eight total rotations. While you are stirring, chant:

Water, Water so clean and clear
Clear all blocks from me and
Take them far away from here
So mote it be

Now get into the water and relax for a it. Breath in deeply and allow the orange scent to fill you. After soaking for a bit, start to wash your body and chant or sing as you imagine a bright orange glow:

Lovely Goddess of the water
Assist me here and now
to clear all blocks
to my prosperity
Wash away all dirt
and psychic grim
and open the way for me
to be prosperous

It's okay to have the chant written down to read while you wash your body.

After you get out of the tub and dry off. Take the orange slices and use them put them in your garbage disposal and as you grind them up imagine all blocks being chomped away.

Luci' Wealthy Boeheim Money Pouch

This is an email I received from Grace that created her own Wealthy Bohemian Pouch:

"Luci, I wanted to share this with you...last week I had an event to do. I put it out there to the Universe that I wanted abundance around this event. I said: 'I am open to all the abundance the Universe has for me. I welcome abundance with open arms in gratitude and JOY.' It worked! The lady who was paying me not only paid me for the event but gave me three times more than I asked for. Yes, three times. Gratitude! JOY! Abundance!"

Items you will need:

1. One small- to medium-sized pouch or sack, preferably with a drawstring or some other mechanism to close the top. Or, If you prefer, you can use your favorite fabric and use a ribbon to tie the top closed.

2. A pinch or two of Kitchen herbs –

   Three of any combination of the following:

   cinnamon (ground or a tiny stick), nutmeg, any type of mint, basil, oregano, bay leaf, clove, rosemary, thyme, ginger (powered), or anything else you feel inspired to use

   You can also use herbal tea bags such as Mexican 7 herb tea (you would only use one of these and nothing else), chamomile, peppermint, and/or anything that makes you feel inspired when you smell it.

3. Three silver coins such as dimes (the older the better, or for extra good luck, ones with your birth year on it).

4. A pen (green ink is the best, but blue or black will do).

5. One small sheet of paper, 3 x 3 inches. Or you can cut it down to size. Any color will do.

6. A one-dollar bill.

7. One or two gemstones or crystals—choose any that inspires you. Suggestions: tigers' eye, aventurine, quartz, agate, emerald, jade, hematite, citrine, any green or orange stone.

8. A safe candle holder, matches or a lighter.

Directions:

Gather the items and schedule about ½ hour to an hour of personal time.

Take a few deep breaths and close your eyes. Imagine what types of things would make you happy if you had all of the money you wanted and were living a prosperous life. Open your arms wide push down. Breathe in the air. Let go of any cares. Allow feelings of being joyful, wealthy, prosperous, and healthy to emerge. If you need to sit, stand, dance, sing, etc., do whatever makes you feel good from the inside out. Put on your favorite songs, the ones that make you want to dance and feel good, if that's what it takes.

a. Now take the green candle. Hold it with the top facing loud: "I bless you and give you the property of wealth and prosperity. As you burn and fade in size so shall my bills and debts subside."

b. Put the candle in its holder and light it.

c. Stare into the flame and imagine that your bills (debt) is now becoming smaller and smaller until they are completely gone. Imagine each debt of yours paid in full. You can also write this on the receipt, in your registry if you are using a checking account, etc. Have fun with this and imagine the freedom you'd feel having zero debt and all of your bills are always paid in full with ease and grace.

d. After blinking and taking in a few deep breaths, then change your focus to replace those bills and debts with more money than you've ever had flowing into your life with more ease and more grace. Get excessive in the amount that flows into your mind's eye. Feel it in your hands, filling up your banking account, increasing your investments, and so on.

e. Imagine being affluent with wealth and prosperity coming to you in leaps and bounds. See yourself dancing with money and imagine that is money being attracted to you. In fact, you are now irresistible to money. Open your arms wide, let money into your life. Allow your emotions to stir, dance, play your favorite happy music, get outlandish in your imagination.

f. Then take the pouch and hold it in your hands in a prayer position. When you start to feel your hands warm up, say: "I bless you and give you the property of wealth and prosperity for myself and for those I share this wealth with."

g. Then take the pouch and hold it in your hands in a prayer position. When you start to feel your hands warm up,

say: "I bless you and give you the property of wealth and prosperity for myself and for those I share this wealth with."

h. Take the pen and paper and write:

Money, Money flow to me

Make it as quick as it can be

Money, Money Flow to me

Make it as quick as it can be

Let this spell not reverse or place upon me any curse

It is safe for me to be affluent, wealthy, healthy, and happy.

I now open the floodgates to my prosperity and claim my riches here and now!

In Totally Satisfying, Harmonious, and Perfect Ways Under Grace for the Highest Good of All Concerned.

It is Now Done! It is Now So!

I thank thee! I thank thee! I thank thee!

You can leave the candle burning in a safe area until it is completely burned down.

Keep this pouch in a safe place where you will be able to access it easily. You can carry it in your purse or put it inside your car glove compartment, or wherever you will be reminded of it often. If you start to feel fearful about money, take a few deep breaths,

Affirm out loud and in the mirror that It is safe for me to be wealthy." You can also rub the outside of your pouch. It is best you not let others play with this pouch, as some people may become jealous when your life starts to become prosperous.

i. Start placing each item into your pouch. The order does not matter, but what does matter is that you hold each item in your dominant hand and bless it. Say the following for each item:

Dimes- "I bless you to flow abundantly into my life"

Gems – I bless you to ground my spell

Paper—(folding it towards you into thirds) "I bless you to send my command and return wealth back to me."

Herbs—"I bless you to speed my request."

Dollar bill—"I bless you with divine love to bring to me great riches and wealth from above."

Once you have placed everything (except the candle) inside the pouch, hold it to your heart and say, "I bless this pouch with Divine Love to bring to me that which is mine by divine right. With harm to none, not even myself." At this point you can add "In the name of" whatever being feels right for you—Jesus or the universe or the Lord, the God of My Being, etc. There is no right or wrong way you can do this.

Done! I thank thee! I thank thee! I thank thee!

You can leave the candle burning until it is gone. If you need to

Keep this pouch in a safe place where you will be able to access it easily. You can carry it in your purse or put it inside your car glove compartment, or wherever you will be reminded of it often. If you start to feel fearful about money, take a few deep breaths,

now. It is safe for me to be wealthy." You can also rub the outside of your pouch. It is best you not let others play with this pouch, as some people may become jealous when your life starts to become prosperous.

Various Money Spells from various places and creators:

Candle Magic Money Spell

This basic candle magic spell will help draw to you money and wealth. You can use this spell as often as you desire. There is no specific time or day, or week or moon cycle.

Items you will need:

Green candle in a safe container
Essential oil that you love

Take the green candle and you can write you name on it. Holding the candle with the tip next to your belly area by your solar plexus, put a drop of oil on the bottom of the candle and start to rub the candle towards you visualizing money and wealth coming to you. This is called anointing the candle. As a personal note, if you were trying to release something, you'd rub the candle away from you with the base near your stomach.

After you've anointed the candle, place in a candle holder and ensure it is safe and can not cause a fire.

Now stare at the candle and chant the following three times before lighting it.

Money, Money Flow to me
Make it as quick as it can be
let this spell not reverse
or place upon me
any curse
So mote it be

After you light the candle, focus for about 5 minutes on all the feelings you would have received the money. You can hum or laugh, smile and imagine money in your hands. Filling up your purse or wallet. See Paid in Full on your bills.

Repeat this spell for a total of nine days. It is important to continually visualize the feeling of having all the wealth you desire with each step.

On the ninth day your spell is finished and you can let your candle burn down to the end.

Clean Money Spell

Wash your kitchen sink well and then take all of the paper money out of your wallet. Place the money in the sink and start washing it as you are chanting something like

Bless this money and
all it provides for me
I am washing it clean and now it is
attracted to me

When you are done washing each bill, rinse it well and place on a paper towel.

After you've finished washing all of the money, gently press a clean dry paper towel on it. Finish with pressing with a low setting clothes iron. Then place the money back in your wallet and every time you spend some, instruct it to return back to you multiplied.

Money Mirror Spell

This is a fun way to get to know money better and have fun with it. Tape money on the bathroom mirror and every time you walk past it you can blow it kisses. Rub your fingertips on it. Talk to it as if it's a friend, lover or whatever you want. My friend who worked on her money story for years and honestly thought she had a great money relationship. But found out during one of our conversations that it really wasn't that great. She decided to treat the money she placed on her mirror as a lover. First she started with twenty dollars. And within a few weeks her clients started to pay her with twenty dollar bills. She thought that was weird as they usually used credit cards. She decided to increase the bill on her mirror and used a hundred bills. This only took three weeks before her clients started to pay her with hundred dollar bills. She went from doing alright to having to double her rates to keep up with client demands.

If you've had fun working these money spells, you can do an internet search and find hundreds of ideas and spells. Youtube has a lot of them too. I love getting kits, making up my own and doing chants. I look for wealth vibes that have positive affirmations or use mind movies too. The way to create is completely up to you. Let your imagination run wild.

Notes: ✍

Chapter 13

BUILDING WEALTH CONSCIOUSNESS

Now that you know what your wealth consciousness around money was growing up and you have destroyed the Money Boogieman, it is time to close the emotional distance between your deep inner core beliefs regarding the money stories you grew up with and where you want to go from here.

Do an internet search for images that depict an overabundance of money or financial wealth. Look at these pictures and journal how you feel about them now. If you feel upset, cringe or still have some feelings of being offended, go back to destroying your Money Boogieman section, add these feelings to it, and follow the steps over again. From there, ask for money to forgive you and forgive yourself for all the ways you used to deter it from flowing to you. Next, look at the quick five-step process I will share with you next, write them out, and post them on a wall where you can read them often.

Doing this quick five-step process over and over again, you will build a positive wealth consciousness:

Step 1: Make a firm decision and state firmly: "I am ready to get off the island of lack right now!" Remake this decision every time you catch yourself with a lack mentality. This does not mean that you go out and buy whatever you want. It means you make better financial decisions and you choose to manage your money. This decision will become automatic over time.

Step 2: You must be willing to create a new paradigm regarding your beliefs about money. Make this decision definite and firm. You may need to remind yourself that this new paradigm is your new self, and that your old self is the one that was lacking. Reaffirm this every time you feel the energy-of-lack in your life or you fearful over money and finances.

Step 3: Firmly announce to the Universe that you are now available to experience wealth beyond your wildest dreams, fabulous health, freedoms, true, and more joy than you have ever experienced. State you are ready, willing, able, and fully available to receive money.

Step 4: Take an interest in your finances. You need to know where you are before you can know if you are making progress. Create a money flow system that shows you where your money flow is going. Keep it easy at first, by tracking and writing down all money received and money sent out.

Step 5: What you bless, you manifest. Bless all money that comes in and goes out. Bless all the good in your life. Touch the money or checks that come in and you send out. Look at your online accounts and bless the amounts to grow and multiply. Bless every coin and dollar that you have, physically and electronically.

To start building up your wealth consciousness, I recommend the following:

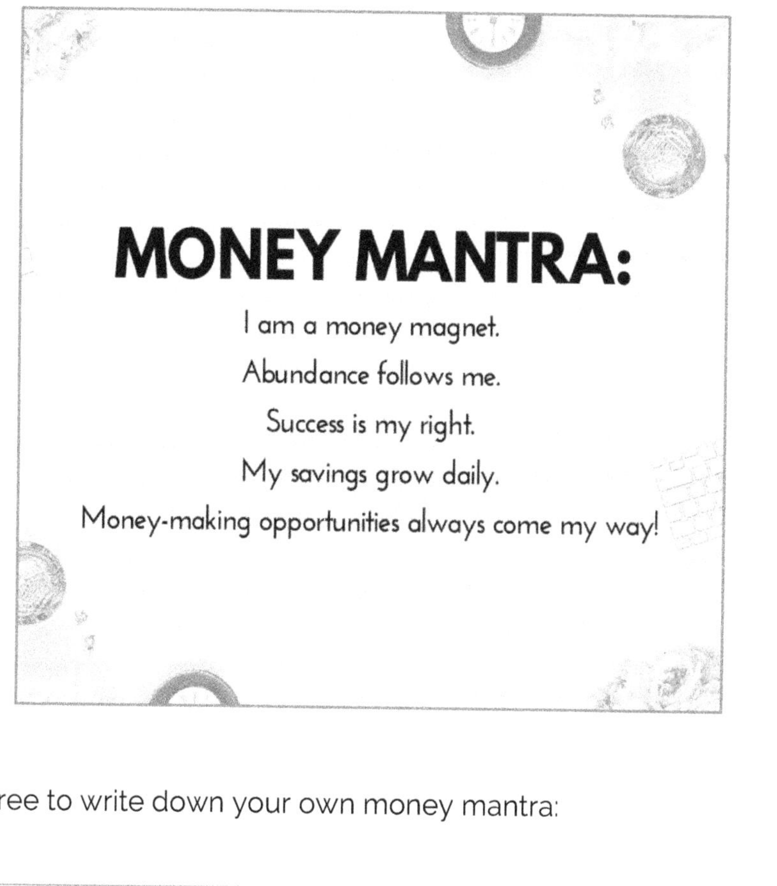

Feel free to write down your own money mantra:

Now, let us create the type of future you truly desire.

Grab your journal and, with a fresh new start, write down all the feelings you want to feel about money from this point forward. As an example, I have written these for you:

I love my fresh new life.

My money wealth springs from all around me, and it fills my life with freedom, joy, and money flow.

Money now supports me and my mission to empower women to become financially independent.

I am so grateful for my money today!

I bless my money every single day.

I love to sing and dance with my money too.

I am grateful that money comes to me in ever increasing amounts and I have money to have, keep and circulate.

Whatever my needs, money is there for me.

As you write down your new beliefs about money, express your new attitude toward money now. How do you perceive money and your wealth consciousness today? Did it spur a new set of money mantras or affirmations that you would like to start using?

Decide today that you will start to mind your own money, tend to your mental money garden, and treat yourself well with random acts of kindness. Prepare yourself for any slippages, so you can "nip them in the bud" right away. Write down at least five things you can do that will make you start believing again in your money flow.

To create a lasting flow of money, it is important that you have a vision for yours. Grab your journal and write down at least one hundred different ways you would like to use money. They can be practical, funny, silly, joyful, adventurous, or creative. Choose anything you like. If money was never and would never be an issue, how exotic would you get? Do not put any limits on these. When you hit a block, take a break and come back to it later. This helps you tap into abundance. You can keep writing your money flow ideas throughout the year if you like. I like to keep mine around, and I add more and more to it. I cross off the ones that have come to pass, some of which I was not expecting. I was flown to Mexico for free for a ten-day retreat that included all my meals. Some of my clients have enjoyed entire vacations without spending a cent. The more you open your mind to more and more wealth consciousness, the more you will experience miracles and magic in your life. Go back and review your journal at least once a week for the first few months. Then, you can look at it once a month if you desire. Add to this all the ways that you would like money to empower you. Call money into your life and affirm that you are available to receive abundance in all forms. When you find pennies, always pick them up and thank the Universe for giving you signs that there is plenty more on its way. When you celebrate the little things, you will grow this into your own personal empire.

Finally, to anchor in your new wealth consciousness and create a new belief around money, take some currency and examine it. Feel its texture; notice how it feels in your hands. Use crisp bills if possible and smell the fresh ink. Close your eyes and use your senses to feel, smell, and touch it. Talk to it as you would talk to a very treasured friend. Treat it well and put it up on the mirror in your bathroom, where you can look at it and touch it every day. As you get to know money and all its facets, you will start to vibrate with your own money vibe. Remember: money does love circulation, so change out your bill on the mirror every month or two. Money embodies giving and receiving. It is your personal experience with money that makes it joyous, or not. Decide which you choose. And when you share money, like when giving tips or buying someone dinner, bless that money to multiply for the gift, the giver, and the receiver.

Are you ready to put what you've learned so far to the test? Let's find out in the next chapter.

Notes: ✍

Chapter 14

21-DAY MAGICAL MONEY MANIFESTATIONS CHALLENGE

In my experience, reading this book alone will not make you fully masterful at being a money magnet or fully creating the life you dream of. It takes practice and self-awareness to maintain your wealth consciousness. So, now it's time to practice what you've learned.

This chapter is completely based on my 21-day Magical Money Manifestation Challenge. It's a workbook, divided into pages for 21 days and with empty spaces which you can fill out to record your responses and track your progress. By taking up this challenge, you will be able to overcome your mental blocks and become financially empowered. Let's begin:

Day 1: Why don't you doodle your thoughts here

	Action Step
Start investing in your EMOTIONAL SELF on a regular basis, no matter how BUSY you are.	Indulge in any ONE of the following activities for 10 to 15 minutes today: Meditation, reading, listening to music, yoga, jogging, or a walk. Use this 'me time' to purge negative emotions, re-energize, and regroup your energies and lay your ground for prosperity.

Day 2: Redefine other boundaries related to your self worth

	Action Step
You are a decent, SELF-RESPECTING, generous, compassionate, KIND-HEARTED woman and you need to draw your boundaries, so that others do not misuse your passion, energy and money.	Sit on the floor in a relaxed posture. Close your eyes and recall a couple of incidents where friends, coworkers, family members misused you. By using your finger, draw an IMAGINARY BOUNDARY around you, meant to keep out manipulative people.

Day 3: Have courage to deal with your negative emotions

<table>
<tr><td>

Your pain, conflict and EMOTIONAL TURMOIL are your energies. Use them correctly, fuel your ambition instead of letting them choke and drown you.

</td><td>

Action Step

Think of a memory or issue that makes you angry and enraged, and then describe it through evocative words and symbols. Now safely burn the paper. As the smoke arises, imagine your pain and sufferings are getting burnt away. It will help you clear away disappointment.

</td></tr>
</table>

Day 4: Replace your inner darkness with light

<table>
<tr><td>

Get rid of anxiety, sadness, and depression as they cast a DARK SHADOW on your soul.

</td><td>

Action Step

Light a candle and look towards it. Look where the self-sabotaging, limiting beliefs and darkness are hiding in your body and soul, and casting a dark mindset. Then imagine a BEAUTIFUL LIGHT penetrating through it and dissolving the darkness with LUMINOSITY.

</td></tr>
</table>

Day 5: Relax your Mind

<table>
<tr><td>

Get rid of negative emotions in your body through conscious body movements, as they are making you ill and blocking POSITIVE energy from flowing inside your body.

</td><td>

Action Step

Sit down in a meditative pose. Focus on spots in your body where NEGATIVE EMOTIONS are stored. Getting rid of all the negative energy accumulated within us is necessary before we can manifest abundant wealth.

</td></tr>
</table>

Day 6: What can you do to find ways to Forgive yourself?

<table>
<tr><td>

FORGIVE yourself: Free yourself from the burdens of the past, regrets, blame and frustrations.

</td><td>

Action Step

Stand in front of the mirror, and place your hand on your heart and say out aloud: "I FORGIVE myself and I am WORTHY of every bit and all of the money the Universe is waiting to send my way." Repeat it at least ten times.

</td></tr>
</table>

Day 7: Come to Terms with your Past

	Action Step
Let go of the desire and guilt of the SITUATIONS in the past, where you wished you had reacted differently or were in more control of your emotions.	Imagine one past situation where you were not in control of yourself and your decisions. ENVISION your younger self surrounded by the conflicting emotions. Now, gently lift your younger self out of the chaos and place it into a safer and securer present. NURTURE it like you nurture a child.

Day 8: Create a magnetic field of positive energies

	Action Step
Grow rich in your thinking, VOCABULARY and outlook.	Get a piece of paper and a marker for this exercise. Write down all the negative words you use daily to describe your current situation on the paper; 'poverty', 'broke', 'cannot afford', 'desperate', 'hopeless', etc. Now start striking them out and start writing POSITIVE WORDS like 'prosperity', 'joy wealth', 'health', and 'abundance'.

Day 9: Look for opportunities which may be a blessing in disguise

	Action Step
Rehearse your responses to situations until you are able to become PROFICIENT with them.	Imagine one past situation where you were not in control of yourself and your decisions. Now imagine the situation again and how you would react in a different and desirable manner. Keep REHEARSING until you encounter a similar situation and are able to respond to it.

Day 10: Find the Positive in Negative situations

	Action Step
There is a hidden POSITIVE in something apparently negative, try to locate it.	Think of a situation in the past where the outcome was not up to your EXPECTATIONS, and you felt disappointed and had to take a different path and journey. Open your mind to the POSSIBILITY that something better came out of it. By doing the other route you might have received something.

Day 11: Offer value to your Money

	Action Step
Figure out ways your work can add value to the world and people's lives, so that the UNIVERSE can compensate you with more OPPORTUNITIES and open the doors to lead you making more money.	Take a sheet of paper and a pen. Draw two boxes. In the first box, list down your skills, talents, PASSIONS, and things that you love doing and are good at. In the 2nd box, write down the ways your special gift and TALENT can help others and make their lives better. For instance, by offering ADVICE to people.

Day 12: Activate your Imagination

	Action Step
Imagine you ALREADY have enough money to fulfill your needs and you are able to ENJOY IT.	When you are worried about money or complaining about not having enough, you have weaker prosperity consciousness and are unable to manifest and attract money. Activate your imagination and your body will respond to it accordingly. Realize how POWERFUL your IMAGINATION is. Harness your desires, dreams, energies and they will turn into reality

Day 13: Cultivate your Mind's Garden

	Action Step
Make your imagination as vivid as possible, as it will allow you to connect to your dreams, tap into the MAGICAL frequency of the Universe where miraculous, wonderful and magical things are being manifested for you.	Close your eyes and imagine that your mind is a lush garden. Now envision all the wonderful things you can grow there. There is a HIDDEN TREASURE here that you have to find.

Day 14: Create beautiful Mental Pictures

	Action Step
Learn to dream big, bold and beautiful. DREAM of things that are normally beyond your reach!	Sit in a relaxed posture. IMAGINE all the finer things you want in life and imagine them in detail. If you want a BIGGER house, think of how many stories and rooms you want it to have. Imagine every tiny detail like the COLOR of the door, and the texture and length of the curtains.

Day 15: Create a Vision Board

	Action Step
Create an ACTUAL map and plan your life, rather than living life on default and on the scraps thrown your way	You will need a journal, some old magazines, a pair of scissors and glue. Create an actual VISION board in the form of a journal. Cut out the pictures of some of your favorite things from the magazines: the places you want to visit, live, and work in, and things you want to wear, eat and EXPERIENCE. You have started a vision board!

Day 16: Manage your Emotional Triggers

	Action Step
Negative thoughts breed negativity; positive thoughts breed POSITIVITY, therefore, one needs to be replaced with another.	Think of a negative thought and you will immediately feel tense, angry and sad. Now, think of a happy thought and you will immediately feel calm, RELAXED and happy. Next, banish negative thoughts out of your mind; literally toss it out by using the eject button. Repeat this exercise with at least two other negative thoughts

Day 17: Use the Power of Positive Affirmations - list your favorites below

	Action Step
Start and end your day by CHANTING positive affirmations.	Take a piece of paper. Write down one positive affirmation like: "I love money; money loves me!" Now, come up with at least 5 positive affirmations related to money and your relationship with it. Say each one out aloud at least 5 times.

Day 18: Manifest your Money Vibes

	Action Step
Carry cash in your wallet to pay for things instead of a CREDIT CARD. Look into it often.	Sit in a comfortable pose, close your eyes and imagine that it is RAINING, POURING money into your wallet and into your bank account. In the next step, hold a new dollar bill and feel its crisp texture. Take in the particular smell of the currency. Bless it and save it in your wallet for another upcoming mini-challenge!

Day 19: Manifest your Opportunities

<table>
<tr>
<td>

Have a welcoming attitude in life, not just towards people but also towards ideas, ESPECIALLY IDEAS!

</td>
<td>

Action Step

Imagine your mind is a house; it has a door or portal. Now, open your front door to money, wealth, prosperity, wellness and ABUNDANCE. Anticipate their arrival, welcome them in and show them in. Treat them well, and tell them how much you have anticipated their arrival. Then place a Dollar Bill in a separate area in your wallet affirming that it is creating a magnetic field around your wallet for receiving more than giving out.

</td>
</tr>
</table>

Day 20: Remove Negativities from your Mind

<table>
<tr>
<td>

Clear away the negativities in your mind. They are like weeds, taking up space and sucking out your ENERGY.

</td>
<td>

Action Step

Imagine again your mind as a garden: There is some wanted growth here but also lots of unwanted one in the shape of weeds. You don't think of them much, but they are sucking out the fertility of your mind. Envision yourself PLUCKING OUT these weeds from your garden and replacing them with useful herbs and fruit yielding plants. Concentrate on the imagery of you NURTURING your plants, and enjoying the BOUNTIES of your fruits and yields.

</td>
</tr>
</table>

Day 21: Send a Generous Vibe Out in the Universe

<table>
<tr>
<td>

Constantly telling others that you don't have enough to spare, makes you subconsciously start believing it and sending a negative message to the Universe. BE GENEROUS with your words and kindness in your actions. You have more than enough kind words and actions.

If someone wants money, state that you've allocated money for other things that you need to attend to.

</td>
<td>

Action Step

Take money out of your wallet. Add more if you can afford to. BLESS this money with prosperity, serenity and generosity. Then give it away, as a gift or as a tip. Give it to someone that needs it genuinely, with a smile. And the Universe would return the favor in other forms.

</td>
</tr>
</table>

Chapter 15

SPEEDING UP THE PROCESS OF MANIFESTATION

By now, I hope you have understood everything and are ready to take things to the next level. In this chapter, I will discuss some things which will help you in speeding up the process of manifestation. Have you ever thought about how it takes a long time to manifest some things that you truly desire in your life and wondered how you can speed up that process?

As an ending note of this book, I am going to share with you some tips and strategies that you can use on your own.

Understanding the Laws of Manifestation and Attraction

The law of attraction is only one single law of quantum physics that can help you manifest the type of lifestyle that you desire, the type of business that you want or take charge as an employee-preneur for the well-being of the company you are working for.

Breaking Down the Law of Germination and How it Applies to Manifestation

It's important to understand the law of germination as it directly affects the law of attraction. According to this law, it takes a certain amount of time for things to happen and, in a lot of cases, that process can be made faster. As an example, let's say you are planting a certain type of plant in your backyard. In my case, I'm planting clumping bamboos. I have two choices: I can either grow it really fast and really tall (up to 25 feet) or I can allow it to grow naturally at a moderate rate so that it's 10 to 12 feet tall. Now, the only difference is that if I wanted it to grow up to 25 feet tall, I'd have to add a little bit of something to the soil in order for it to get to that height. On the other hand, if I didn't want it to be 25 feet tall, then I would add nothing. This is the basic idea of the law of germination – there are certain things that you can do to make the process of manifestation faster.

What to Do Next

One of the very first things to do in order for you to move faster is to slow down and take some breaks to recharge, rejuvenate, and allow the energies to process. The seed represents the idea which you are "planting," whereas adding something to the soil, such as the efforts of watering, tendering, and pulling out the weeds, encompasses creating the right circumstances for the desired results to appear.

Let's say you want to manifest a car in your life, but you don't have enough money in your bank account. You then have to ask yourself, how do I manifest either the car itself, the money to buy it, or the circumstances that allow me to drive the car without having to have to pay for the insurance, maintenance or gas? Not a lot of people think about the third option. They think that in order to achieve something, they need to do the work and it will show up automatically. But, by doing so, they're not opening the doorways to understanding that it is not showing up in the way that they expect it to. If you remove some of the blinders, you will be able to start looking at other opportunities that might lead to things even better than what you hoped for. What this means is that it will open the gateways which the universe can use to give you something even better.

It's even more exciting and when you sit back, put your fingers together and the tip of your tongue on the roof of your mouth and start imagining:how you would feel to have a car in your life; what it feels like when you're driving it; how it goes around the curves or turns; whether it goes on the highway smooth as silk; how it feels when you're going fast; and so on. Then, ask yourself: Is it quiet inside or is it all kinds of crazy?And if it is the latter, the things which you're trying to create are in the midst of chaos. And if they are in the midst of chaos, you need to realize how you can utilize that chaos to start pulling in the energies to make this manifestation happen faster.

Sit back, meditate on it, and think about how it feels inside of you. You have the laws of attraction and germination, which will help you remove the blinders so that you can clearly see the opportunities which the universe is bringing to your doorstep. When you start balancing things, you also start creating the elixir of true alchemy.

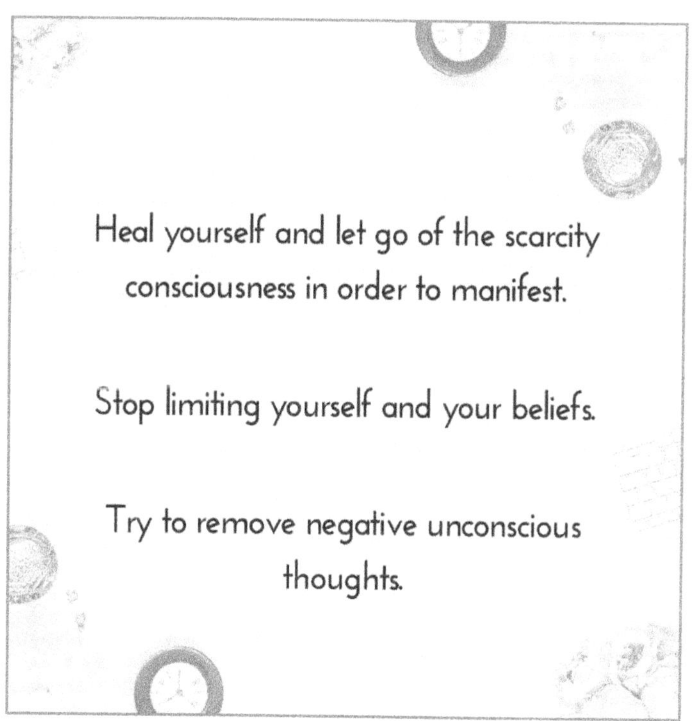

Notes:

Afterward: What is Next?

Creating magical money manifestations is the beginning of your new prosperous future. By reading this book, you have begun to activate your wealth codes, and you will start to see the world differently from this point forward. You will have greater moments of freedom and joy, while increasing your money flow. When you see money as a medium for an energy exchange, you are able to be friendlier toward yourself and money. Catch and transform any money stories that are hindering you and your place, and you will be able to tap into your ultimate and full wealth potential. The Universe is an ever-abundant place. There has never been a time in history where one single person can create a massive money movement. Today, there are more ways to make money with more ease and more grace than ever before.

Utilize this book as you need to. You can use it as a reference book. You can make it your own by using markers, post-it notes, and highlighters. As you reread sections of this book, you will notice different words and things that you did not notice before. This is because, as you awaken to your true wealth potential, you recognize things that were hidden to you previously. Rereading and going through the exercises in this book again a few months after the first time, will yield you even more powerful results.

Even though you have finished reading this book, our journey can continue. As you have processed the ideas in this book, you are becoming more attracted to being a money magnet. The more you integrate the processes in this book, the more you will have more money, freedom, and joy in your life.

WHAT OTHER PEOPLE ARE SAYING ABOUT LUCI

"Luci helped me become clear and taught me how to allow everything to unfold gracefully. She took me step by step so I never felt like it was overwhelming in the process. Her process helped me to become much stronger and clearer with my life's purpose. I would say that Luci is incredible because she really sees you as who you really are and beyond, she can see who you really are, and bring it out of you in a safe loving environment, there is no judging or blaming only love and compassion. Luci is the perfect mentor. Her unique solution is incredible because it wasn't invasive or weak, it was so powerful and at the same time soothing and gentle. She is like Gandalf with silk gloves. In summary, my experience was intense and at the same time gentle and deep, it's like reaching out to all the angles of the soul and healing one by one. Now I'm learning how to use my inner magic, and how to expand spiritually."
~ Roni Diaz

"When I'm talking to Luci, I feel like the Universe is talking to me through her. She is able to draw out of me what really lights me up. We explore this, and she has an ear to pull out the precise words that allow me to articulate precisely how I feel and how I can use this for my copywriting! Plus how to get fabulous testimonies too! Luci is a game changer, and she guides me to know what my next step toward success is. This next step comes from a deeper inner place from within me. After each call I feel that she has helped me build an inner strength, and I always feel like I have faith that I can do it." ~ Joia Jitahidi

"Before having a Blessing Prayer and coaching session with Luci, I had been experiencing a large amount of fear around doing my first retreat. I had reached out to my family, friends, and coaches, all were encouraging and yet the fear remained. After having this one session with Luci, the fear subsided and I began to look forward to my retreat. In truth, I didn't know exactly how to describe this session, only that there were things Luci knew that I hadn't shared on the phone call (examples – that I lock my knees often and that I grip with my toes), that after the session my fear had subsided, and that overall I felt lighter and more energized. After my retreat, I signed up for the only retreat member who was not already on my program. As frightened as I was about my retreat, what I discovered was that it was as easy as breathing. Each participant got from the experience everything I intended for them to receive and more."
~Audrey Pyon

"Luci wasn't afraid to deal with heavy issues. Money issues are usually linked to problematic or traumatic events from one's past, and it's as though Luci knew what to say. I also appreciate that she never gave up on me, even when I wanted to. She combined Karma clearing with practical, proven advice. And she is very bold in expressing the importance of your spiritual work, in tandem with the practical side.

Bottom Line: If you feel like you're stuck in a financial quagmire, call Luci now! Her approach to helping people with money breakthroughs is legit. I went from practically trying to throw my money away to being in the flow. I now know my life purpose, I have people approaching me for speaking gigs, just published a book, and I feel very blessed to be where I am. Thank you Luci for believing in me, even when I couldn't." ~ Earl J. Katigbak

Posted on Facebook by Cindia:

"Okay, THAT was fun! I love my work for many reasons, and a top one is because of how it connects me with really fascinating people on a daily basis, and today was no exception. I was in my first conversation with Luci McMonagle, and she said that people make money when they talk to her. I liked that idea, and I don't want to say I was skeptical, but there was a part of me that was hoping it was TRUE! Guess what? Mid-conversation, Groom comes into the room and places our van title in front of me with a pen to sign. He had JUST put it up for sale, and a guy stopped, looked at it, and had cash in pocket. Deal done. So yes, while I was talking to her, money came in."

A Note from the Author

Thank you for upgrading your life and choosing to improve your life and the life of those you will share your life with. I am deeply and profoundly proud you have decided to take the opportunity to change your life from the inside out.

I am sending you blessings and healings for your future to be in alignment with your true hearts' desires. You are now apart of my community and I am here for you.

Abundant Blessings,

Luci McMonagle

Notes:

CPSIA information can be obtained
at www.ICGtesting.com
Printed in the USA
FFHW020658291219
57322117-62826FF